CREATED

IN THE IMAGE OF

GOD

A Foundational Course
in the Kabbalah

Rabbi Esther Ben-Toviya, M.A.

First published by O Books, 2007
O Books is an imprint of John Hunt Publishing Ltd.,
The Bothy, Deershot Lodge, Park Lane, Ropley, Hants, SO24 0BE, UK
office1@o-books.net
www.o-books.net

Distribution in:

UK and Europe
Orca Book Services
orders@orcabookservices.co.uk
Tel: 01202 665432 Fax: 01202 666219 Int. code (44)

USA and Canada
NBN
custserv@nbnbooks.com
Tel: 1 800 462 6420 Fax: 1 800 338 4550

Australia and New Zealand
Brumby Books
sales@brumbybooks.com.au
Tel: 61 3 9761 5535 Fax: 61 3 9761 7095

Far East (offices in Singapore, Thailand, Hong Kong, Taiwan)
Pansing Distribution Pte Ltd
kemal@pansing.com
Tel: 65 6319 9939 Fax: 65 6462 5761

South Africa
Alternative Books
altbook@peterhyde.co.za
Tel: 021 447 5300 Fax: 021 447 1430

Text copyright Esther Ben-Toviya 2007

Design: Stuart Davies

ISBN-13: 978 1 84694 007 1
ISBN-10: 1 84694 007 9

A CIP catalogue record for this book is available from the British Library.

Printed in the US by Maple Vail

CREATED

IN THE IMAGE OF

GOD

A Foundational Course
in the Kabbalah

Rabbi Esther Ben-Toviya, M.A.

BOOKS

Winchester, UK
Washington, USA

Dedicated to:

"My Beloved"

Contents

Acknowledgements

How do we acknowledge the myriads of people who enter our lives daily, influence us for the ultimate unfolding of our Souls, and leave their imprint of love upon our hearts? I can only say thank you to you who have shared yourselves with me generously, and helped me become fully who I Am. It is the dynamic unfolding of God, each time we hug one another.

I acknowledge my children, my parents, my siblings and my teachers, my mentors, my friends and my students/patients. I cannot name one from the other, for so often you have each engaged in all of these relationships with me in my Life. My children are my friends, parents, at times, and teachers. My students are at the same time my teachers. I have had friends who are parents, sisters and brothers to me and I have been gifted with special teachers who have been parent/friend/child to me. It is all God.

While this book is based in the mysticism of the Kabbalah, the writing of this book, the explanations of information, wisdom and the love contained herein have come from my beloved Archangels, especially Archangel MichaEL, who share the wisdom of Heaven with me for the Light to shine more fully in the hearts of those here on this planet. I am grateful and humbled to be a part of it, merely the vessel whose fingers type the keys, with hopes of transparency that the Higher Truth shine more purely as it flows through. I am a part. I am grateful for that part.

Abbreviation Guide

I use abbreviations for the ease of language. If you learn the abbreviations as you progress through the text it will increase your ability to converse using these new terms.

Authentic Soul   **AS**   Eternal Being in the Higher Dimensions

Incarnate Self   **IS**   Finite Person in this Lifetime

Infinite Worlds

   Infinite Atzilut   IA   Emanation, the place of Oneness

   Infinite B'riyah   IB   Power of Intellect, World of Thought

   Infinite Yetzirah   IY   Power of Emotions, World of Feeling

Finite Worlds

   Spiritual Assiyah   SA   Mind, Thoughts and Feelings incarnate

   Physical Assiyah   PA   Physical body

Hebrew Pronunciation Key

Hebrew is written in characters which are different from the English alphabet characters and some letters are pronounced with sounds that are not in the English alphabet. Hebrew is read right to left. For ease of reading I have transliterated the Hebrew words in this book, which means Hebrews words are written phonetically using English letters. Transliterated Hebrew words may vary in spellings; for example, you may see the winter holiday the Feast of Dedication written as: Hanukkah, Chanukah, Hannukah, in the public domain. There is no one set rule for spelling words in English which are written in different characters in the original language. The following guide will provide the reader with the closest pronunciation of Hebrew sounds in English:

The accent **generally** falls on the last syllable:

Sha-BBAT

Me-no-RAH

To-RAH

"Ch" is the Hebrew letter, *chaf*, and is a guttural sound in the back of the throat as in "Bach". Note: It is never pronounced like the "ch" in "chair"

"Tz" is the letter *tzadee*, and is pronounced as in "pizza" and "matzah".

"Kh" is the Hebrew letter *het*, and is a softly aspirated "h" sound To indicate a word is Hebrew I have italicized it the first time it appears in the text. Thereafter it will appear in normal format for ease of reading.

I use the English letters **YHVH** to indicate where the Hebrew text uses the ineffable or unspoken name of God. **YHVH** stands for the Hebrew letters *Yod, Hey, Vav, Hey*. **YHVH** is the emanating "Breath of Life" or "Power-flow of Life" aspect of God that is usually translated "Lord" in the King James Version Bible. I translate **YHVH** as "The Holy One". In the Kabbalah **YHVH** is "breathed" not spoken.

Introduction

Welcome to *Created In The Image of God – A Foundational Course in the Kabbalah.* I am so glad you are giving the gift of love to your Self by reading these pages and doing the exercises in the Journey Pages. From this moment your Life will never be the same.

Shoes That Don't Fit

My younger sister, Elizabeth, was staying in my home one time while exploring the possibility of moving to the city in which I was living. She found an apartment, applied to the college in the area and found a job that would help her with expenses. Things seemed to be falling together for her. I was thrilled to have her there so close! But one day she came to me and told me she just couldn't stay there. She needed to go back to her home state. "I feel like I have my shoes on the wrong feet. They are my shoes, but they are on the wrong feet!" she said. "This is just not the right place for me. I know you are disappointed, but, I can't stay here." I was disappointed, but I understood the wisdom of her words.

Wearing the shoes that fit in your Life is an important thing. You need to have shoes that fit according to the pathway you walk in Life.

Have you ever had a pair of shoes that just did not quite fit? No matter how short of a time you tried to wear them, they ended up hurting your feet? Are there shoes that sit in your closet year after year because cute as they may be, they cause your feet to hurt if you wear them for any length of time? Do you have any shoes that pinch your toes, make you walk funny, hurt you arches, are too loose on your heel, or cramp your bunion? Have you ever had a pair like that? No matter how hard you try some shoes just won't adjust to the shape and size of your feet!

If you are wearing them now, take them off. TAKE THEM OFF – RIGHT NOW! If they are in your closet, go put them in the "give away" bag. NOW!

Congratulations! You have taken the first step of staying in your integrity and allowing yourself to be who you truly are comfortably, **Created In The Image Of God!**

Your shoes symbolize the garments you put on your feet to walk your pathway. Your feet desire to walk the path true and sure. Anything that is inauthentic to that walk is inauthentic to you! Let your feet enjoy total freedom for the rest of your Life – and never put those shoes back on. However cute, expensive or dear it is to you – let go of that which is inauthentic to your Life and your pathway in this Lifetime will become a joy for you to walk – jump, run, and exult in. Choose some shoes that you feel good in and your feet will thank you. Choose that in Life which is truly you and your Authentic Soul will thank you!

Now you have begun your journey to discover your Self created in the image of God! You will find that this is a process of Lifelong learning. You are just beginning to build a framework that will serve you for the rest of your Life. As you apply the principles within these pages the framework you build will give you a reference point from which you will be better able to make decisions that keep you in your Path of Peace. It does not exclude what you have already learned. It helps you bring together with continuity that which you have learned. The principles you learn will create a matrix of understanding to which you will be able to add future information. This matrix will give you a center to dwell in that is deep within you. This center is a place of serenity which is not swayed by what is happening in the external because you will be motivated internally. As things change in your Life on the outside you will be able to keep your balance from the inside. That gives you a place of harmony and balance regardless of how chaotic Life may become. This gives you the ability to use all parts of your Soul and the Four Worlds (from the Kabbalah) within you to stay in harmony and balance regardless of your circumstances.

In the first chapter, *Undifferentiated and Differentiated Being*, some of the concepts are very esoteric and abstract. You may feel you are putting your brain out on a stem to conceive of what is being described. These "mental gymnastics" will serve to open your consciousness and increase your mental energy. It may take some time to bring an understanding up from your unconscious "memory" to your conscious, waking mind. The more you use the practices and principles given the more illumination you bring to your understanding. You are expanding your consciousness.

In the chapters on the differences between your Authentic Soul and your Incarnate Self and the meditations you may be doing more fact finding and information gathering, especially about your own Being. By the time you finish this book you will find that your ability to understand and utilize the esoteric concepts in the first chapter will have increased greatly. You will have increased your vocabulary and ability to express yourself in spiritual terms of the indescribable, as well. You will have joined with our ancestors in the journey of seeking out and receiving (Kabbalah) the mysteries of this vast Universe, and beyond.

There are journal pages that you can fill in with your own unique information and inspirational thoughts to aid you in your quest. Some pages of the journal are blank – because that is your canvas to paint from the unique experience you have with your own Being. On other pages you will find questions that lead you to find the answers from within your Being. The answers to these open door questions are neither right nor wrong. They are simply your answers.

As you integrate the wisdom and these foundational concepts of the Kabbalah you will begin to manifest Life experiences (consciously and unconsciously) in which you can practice and put to work what you are learning. The "framework" will be building, moving and shaping within you. Watch for the Life messages within those experiences, for they will guide you in wisdom and confirm for you the changes you are undergoing.

At the end of the book is a section called "Angel Wisdoms" for they are inspired messages from the angels to guide you in wisdoms for living. Try using these thirty-one meditations for focus on a daily basis for a month. At the end of the month start over, and see how these wisdoms begin to manifest in your Life. If you begin using them on the 5th day of the month, begin with the 5th Angel Wisdom so that you are in sync with the thirty-one wisdoms. The thirty-first wisdom is at the very end, and can be used in partnership with every day, or for the last day in those months with thirty-one days.

If you read the Wisdoms all at one sitting you will not receive the same benefit as you will when you focus on them individually day by day. As you read the Wisdom you will have thoughts about it, feelings may emerge about it, but as you use it in meditation you will transcend your thoughts and feelings and receive the *sod*, the hidden and secret meaning that is especially for you at this particular time in your Life. They are timely to the moment you are using them. That is why they can be used over and over again, for they become fresh in the moment of Now. As you ask your Inner Guidance, or your angels questions that arise about the Wisdom you will "hear" their answers in the quiet of your mind; you will engage in an inter-dimensional "Eternal Dialogue". The angels may remind you of that day's focus Wisdom when something happens during the day which relates to the Angel Wisdom you used that morning. It becomes a dialogue between your everyday Life and the Eternal. It is an open door to walk through for dialogue with the Divine.

The Message of the Redwood Tree

Once when I was meditating at the foot of the largest tree in a forest of great Redwoods in California I was taken by and in awe of the immensity of that wonderful tree. It was so grand and yet so friendly feeling. I couldn't even see to the top of it. I had to use the zoom lens of my video camera to begin to see the top branches. As I continued to meditate upon this magnificent tree and the energy coursing through it I began to feel its root system; how deeply they went and how far out the roots expanded mingling with the roots of other trees around it. The breadth of roots anchored it and nurtured it in Mother Earth. As I was sitting in awe of it I heard its tree Voice speak to me:

"If you could see all of your Lifetimes and your Eternal Soul you would see that you are greater than me."

That message made me stop and realize that whatever Lifetimes I have had or will have are all part of this enormous, expansive energy that is me, my Authentic Soul, all part of the Eternal Soul placed within me. What deeper wisdom was the consciousness in that tree tapping into? What ancient mystery was he revealing? This wonderful tree could "see" and experience my Energy – my Authentic Soul – not just my body, my voice, but my vibrations, my tuning, my harmonics, my

Being as an emanation of God; parts of me that I don't see. This tree was a sentient intelligence that was experiencing me as I was experiencing it. I am used to talking to the trees as I hike through the woods, and speaking to my plants, and I have been talking with animals since I was a child, but, to have a tree say something so profound to me was a new experience for me. That is what this book is about; connecting to the Eternal Being that is the core of each of us; the Authentic Soul that this Redwood Tree saw in me which was more than my physical presence.

In mysticism from around the world, trees are used as an axis mundi, a Latin term which means, according to the Merriam-Webster dictionary, the "turning point of the world: line through the earth's center around which the universe revolves". In mysticism it is that symbolic axis or pole of energy that connects the Heavens or Higher Dimensions and the Earth plane, and it extends through the Dimensions. In the physical world, trees are a physical manifestation of the axis mundi because their leaves reach up to the sunlight and turn the sunlight into energy, food for the tree, and the roots reach deep into Mother Earth, drinking in the sweet waters and nourishing the tree from the ground. The roots stabilize the tree so it can grow taller and reach out wider with its branches while anchoring it that it be not blown over by the wind. It stabilizes the ground and keeps the soil from eroding. It bears fruit for others on the Earth. It provides cooling shade. Because trees are an axis mundi, they are powerful prisms for transcendence in meditation. Tree meditations can be powerful for transcendence and grounding, bearing fruit in your Life, abundance, and stability. I invite you to sit near a tree sometime and begin your meditation by simply opening your senses to the energy coursing through the tree. Your meditation will take a Life and story of its own from there!

Your Authentic Soul - larger than that great Redwood is what you will explore in this foundational course of the Kabbalah. You will not be the same when you finish this book as you are right now at its beginning. There will be an expansiveness added to your ability to conceive and receive inspiration.

You may become hungry to spend some time alone and reflect upon some of the concepts that light your pathway. You may feel you want to stop working and go to a sanctuary and truly move into the deeper meanings which are dawning upon your mind and heart. Give yourself that gift of a little retreat whether it is one day or two days, or even an afternoon; whether you actually go somewhere away from home or go on a day retreat to your back yard or a favorite park. If you do not see how you can afford to take this time in your busy Life lift this concern up to your angels and say something like, "I am willing to make this change in my Life, please show me some options of how to take this time off for my Self. Please show me how and suggest where would be best to go." When it comes to making changes in your Life remember the liberating words of Louise Hay, "...you do not need to know how... all you need is to be willing." The Universe has a wonderful way of supporting us in our intentions when they are sincere! You will find that a way or opportunity will open up for you in your schedule and it will be up to you to take advantage of it.

Some of the effects of the consciousness shifts will show up immediately in the events of your Life. Some effects will be gradual and slow. But, from this time forward, you will have gained a new consciousness of your Self; a new aspect of your Being; an aspect that is centered and grounded. A "you" that is empowered to fly as high as you have always known you can in your deepest and most secret desires. You will have a more complete concept of your Incarnate Self, who you are in your personality and characteristics in this Life and your Authentic Soul, your Eternal Being in the Dimensions outside of time and space, the Higher Dimensions.

There are no demands of what you must believe or not believe within these pages; there are no boundaries. There are no demands that you adhere to a strict code of thinking or that you unlearn what your Soul has followed until now. You can integrate what you have already learned in Life and what serves your Soul's purposes in this Lifetime into the framework that you will weave in your consciousness as you read these pages. It is expansive, it is inclusive. The basic concepts of this book are coming from the Kabbalah, the mysticism of Abraham, as well as fresh revelation from the Angels. Both the Kabbalah foundations and fresh revelation from the angels are necessary for relevance today. The Kabbalah has been quite fragmented in its popularity currently, so I have included below some background on the Kabbalah, and its relevance to the other sacred writings of the Hebrew traditions. I have included with an understanding of the metaphysical need for fresh revelations.

The Kabbalah – The Receiving

The Kabbalah means "the receiving". It is a spiritual pathway of transcendence from Abraham, dating back nearly 4,000 years. He brought it with him as he left Ur of Chaldees. It includes theoretical concepts of creation in very metaphysical terms of multiple Dimensions and the created Beings of those Dimensions (angels, for example), our interaction with them and theirs with us, spiritual practices for living in harmony in this Dimension and transcendence to Higher Dimensions for the purpose of bringing a Higher Light back to this Dimension; the meditations, and ecstatic practices are for transcendence, as well. These practices and concepts were handed down from Abraham, to Isaac, Jacob, and Joseph, orally; which is "the receiving", Kabbalah. They continued to develop throughout history and we see them surface in personalities such as Moses (channeled, or received the *Torah*, Genesis, Exodus, Leviticus, Numbers, Deuteronomy), King David and King Solomon (wrote wisdom scriptures) and the Prophets (who "received" prophecy through the *Ruach HaKodesh*, Holy Spirit). We see these practices in the New Testament stories of Angel visitations and healing practices.

But those who practiced the mysticism of Abraham were not always called "Kabbalists". At different times they were called by different names such as "Those Who Know", "The Reapers of the Field", "Companions in the Light", "Masters of Mystery", "Men of Belief", "Masters of Knowledge", "Those Who Know Grace", "Children of Faith", "Children of the King's Palace", "Those Who Know Wisdom", "Those Who Have Entered and Left".

Throughout the Kabbalah the Angels, *malachim*, which means "messengers" bring messages and information, transferring the Divine Plenty through the Dimensions, and they carry messages back up to the Higher Dimensions, to the Throne Room, as the Kabbalah metaphorically calls the place before The Holy Presence of the Most High. Throughout the Kabbalah the angels bring to humanity fresh revelation, as does the Ruach HaKodesh, the Holy Spirit.

The Kabbalah is not a golden thread of spiritualism that is woven throughout the Torah, (the first five books of the Bible; Genesis through Deuteronomy) rather it is the heart and soul of the Hebrew traditions. While the Torah is the body of sacred writings which teach us our sacred history and sacred ways to live in harmony, it is also a "distillation" of the deeper truths hidden within the Kabbalah. Torah can be translated "the Light-Bearer" for the root within it is *Or*, which means Light. The Torah is written in very symbolic language which is not understood within a literal reading of the text. Those seeking God and wisdom studied the Torah and asked questions and gave answers – many answers – which were memorized and continually handed down generation to generation. Finally, by the 2nd century CE, a wise rabbi, Judah HaNasi (The Prince) said that if we didn't write it down it would be lost. So the discussions of the Torah, which had gone on orally for centuries was written down. Then the discussions continued, on both the Torah, and the previous discussions on the Torah, which by then were called the *Mishnah* (from the root for "second"). The new discussions were also written down, century upon century until about the 6th century at which time they were closed. These new discussions were called the *Gamara* (from the root for "finish, completion"). Together, the Mishnah and Gamara are called the *Talmud* (from the root "learning"). Remember, the spiritualism of the Kabbalah is at the heart of all of these sacred texts. As you experience more of the transcendence of the Kabbalah (Receiving) you understand to a deeper truth and wisdom the Torah and the Talmud. But, the discussions did not stop there. Throughout the centuries since, there have been commentaries written on the Torah, Talmud, and commentaries on the commentaries. Meanwhile, the Kabbalah has remained for the most part, secretive. As with any system that empowers the individual, it has been hidden for reasons of political threat at varying times in history. It has been secretly practiced and handed down from teacher to student for centuries and millennia.

Parts of the Kabbalah have been written down at varying times. One of the most powerful and mysterious books of Kabbalah is Sefer

Yetzirah, the Book of Creation. It is not known with certainty when this text was written down; however, it is thought to have existed in Biblical times due to commentaries and the Talmud referring to it. In the last sentences of Sefer Yetzirah it says, "When Abraham, our father.... looked and probed (meditative journey) .... he was successful in Creation." This direct reference to Abraham links him to the origins of the practices. A hand written manuscript of Sefer Yetzirah, which is in the British Museum, says under the title "This is the book of the Letters of Abraham our father, which is called Sefer Yetzirah, and when one gazes (*tzafah*) into it, there is no limit to his wisdom." The Sefer Yetzirah is filled with meditative portals for drawing down wisdom, using the Hebrew letters, angels, planets and their energy, and creating Life.

Another very informative and powerful book is the Bahir (Bright, Clear). It gives us information about the *Shekinah*, the feminine aspect of God in this Dimension. And the most commonly mentioned (and possibly least understood), is the Zohar (Bright). The Zohar teaches about the Creation, Sephirot, and Dimensions integrating with this world.

Kabbalah denotes action; it is not a noun; it is derived from the word *kibel*, to receive. Therefore, you can expect that learning Kabbalistic concepts is an action oriented process. The foundations of the Kabbalah, which you will learn in Created In The Image of God, ground you in who you are in the physical world and in the larger framework of the Higher Dimensions. It is the "You are here" arrow on the road map of your Life. Without that arrow a map does little good, for you have no point of reference. This is foundational to understanding the rest of the Kabbalah, and growing in wisdom and in truth. To bring relevance for the energy of the planet today the wisdom is given through "fresh angelic revelation".

Fresh revelation for "now" is necessary because the Kabbalah is a dynamic and unfolding development of enlightenment. The energy of the Earth 4,000 years ago was at a certain vibrational and textural energy, however, it changes and develops over the centuries and millennia. The energy and collective consciousness of the planet is different than it was thousands of years ago. So too, in each age, the Kabbalah, which simply means "the receiving" will shift with the shift of energy needed to stay in harmony with this Dimension, the physical world, and yet constantly impel it in its journey back toward The Source from which it was emanated. The energy of the consciousness of this Dimension could only sustain a certain level of Light in years past, but it can now sustain a different level of Light through the enlightenment process. The energy of the Earth is different now than it was in Abraham's time. The Light, the Energy, the vibrational texture is different due to the enlightenment of this Dimension in progress. So the Kabbalah is not stagnant, but is dynamically unfolding. We do not discard its foundation, we build upon it. We stand on the shoulders of our ancestors so we can see farther. As we do that those who come after us can stand upon our shoulders and see farther than we can at this time. The concepts, exercises and meditations in this book are rooted and grounded in authentic Kabbalah **and** fresh information that is given within that framework to bring balance.

The paradigm of norm in this Dimension changes and shifts, for that is growth. The information and experiences you will be receiving will help you stay in harmony with that paradigm shift as you learn to stay in harmony with your Authentic Soul, which is outside of time and space of this physical world. You will consciously fulfill this Lifetime as you become more aware of what your Life challenges, soul contracts and gifts to give in this incarnation are all about. You will have access to learn what this Lifetime is about for you, what you are learning, what you are sharing, what you have set an intention to accomplish for your own enlightenment and refinement of Eternal Soul. Wouldn't you love to fulfill this incarnation and actually start on fulfilling the next? It can happen! You can bring in extra Light from above beyond your "contracts" for this Lifetime. The angels call this "extra curricular activity". Collectively that helps all of Creation move higher in the Light, deeper into the enlightenment and the Oneness of all Life.

You are vibrating at a certain level of Light as you begin reading this book. As you finish you will be vibrating at a higher level of Light for the expansion that has happened within you. Always remember that our bodies are not separate from our mind, emotions and spiritual energy. As you change your consciousness you may find your physical needs changing as well. It is normal to need to increase your intake of water to rinse your body well as your energy is heightened. It provides cleansing and a "cool down system" for your cells as you bring in a higher level of Light. You may find certain foods too "dense" feeling for the "lightness" you are experiencing. Eat that which seems to be in harmony with your energy. Some liquids may seem more toxic to you. Follow your inner guidance on making decisions of what to eat and drink and what to delete from your normal diet. Remember, balance, variety and lots of water is always a good guideline. Take time to take deep breaths! The word for breath in Hebrew is *ruah*. The word *ruah* also means spirit. When you breathe deeply you not only oxygenate the cells of your wonderful body, but you also bring inspiration to your mind and hope to your heart. When you breathe deeply you "in-spirit" yourself!

As your Soul prospers under this higher vibration, your body will follow. You will find your body coming into healing and harmony, mirroring your new level of inner strength and contentment.

The **Created In The Image Of God** course includes theoretical learning along with practical applications, rituals, meditative journeys and stories to help you integrate these lessons with fun and ease. The angels remind us that when we are laughing and having fun we raise our vibration level and are able to sustain and emit a higher level of the Divine Light through us. Laughter is a very high level of energy. Have you ever noticed that when Life gets serious or even threatening it very often happens that someone says something humorous and everyone is caught up in the laughter, breaking the tension? It is a way of dealing with the most difficult things in Life. Those most difficult times are so very low in vibrational energy that your Life-force just cannot resonate with it and continue in Life. Humor raises our level of vibrational energy. I saw this very often when I was working in hospice. It was not out of the ordinary for a family member to begin laughing at a deeply emotional or tense moment. It is not out of disrespect or disregard for what is going on, but it is a very human response to that which can be overwhelming if the tension is not changed. That ridiculous comment or joke made at the most tense moment is often referred to by chaplains as "gallows humor", referring to the humor that allows the moment "at the gallows" to pass and to be integrated in a less damaging way. If something difficult happens to you in Life, but something happens that makes you laugh, then the event can more easily be incorporated into your Life in balance. You can accept it. Laughter is a tool our guardian angels often use to help us in the human experience.

While these pages venture into high places and esoteric material you may find you are also brought back to your human experience with thoughts that give you moments of joy and fun, laughter and giggles. There is a new message reaching us that says the Earth is not just a classroom where we come to learn "Life lessons" or a place to work out or balance karma. The Earth is much more! Listen to the message of the Seagull in the following story.

Message of the Seagull

I was lying on the beach on Treasure Island, FL, one afternoon when a flock of seagulls landed near me. I noticed one seagull staring at me rather intently. Every time I looked over at the flock this seagull was still looking over toward me. I realized he was carrying an animal spirit message for me, so I began our conversation by honoring him and thanking him for letting me come and play in his backyard. I recognized that while I was just visiting this beach for a few days, this beach was his home. With a cock to his head he replied to my thoughts with the message,

> "It's all a playground, you know. You humans act as though it is a place to work hard, or to simply learn. It's really a big playground. You learn on the playground, but it is a playground!
> Play! Enjoy this playground!"

That was a big message! I looked at the blue sky mirrored in the blue of the Gulf waves, the fluffy white clouds, the seemingly endless sands, and the people at play. Some were swimming, some sunbathing, some playing ball, and there was a man flying a brilliant, multi-colored row of kites. I saw a grandfatherly looking man holding the hand of a little boy, walking along the edge of the waves. They seemed to illustrate what the seagull was saying, for the grandfather was simply walking along looking ahead, but the little boy was looking around and whistling! He was walking along with a look of enchantment on his face and his lightheartedness was carried in his tuneless whistle. He was having fun on the playground. He was happy, he was content; he had the hand of his tall and sturdy grandfather and he was just happy. The grandfather was just walking with no expression on his face – but the little boy's smile revealed that he got it! He was whistling his Life song. This is what the seagull was saying about what Life can be on this planet. I heard the seagull continue,

"Some of you humans work so hard on the playground you forget why you are here. You are like children who band together in a gang and conspire to boss and bully the other children around with your controls and manipulations. But, it doesn't change the fact that it is a playground. Play on the swings, feel the wind in your hair as you rise high in the sky and then down again only to rise higher the next time! Or play with a partner on the seesaw!"

The seagull continued,

"Sometimes you might feel like sitting under a tree by yourself to read a book, study an ant climbing the tree, or just stare at the sky and imagine what is up there."

I started thinking, "What would my Life be like if instead of thinking 'I have to get up and get to work' I were to think instead, 'I'm getting up to go to play now!'" What if we consider our work as play? Even when we are doing serious work it is a paradigm shift that gives us an

ability to open to the joy of Life, for even on a playground we sometimes go over and put our arm around another child who has been hurt
in some way. But it is still a playground. If you usually have to drag
yourself out of bed when your alarm goes off in the morning, try
replacing your morning thoughts by saying "Now I am going to get up
and go play." See that day as an opportunity of unequaled joy to go
and play; an opportunity once more to see the color green on a bush,
to smell a flower, to hear the voice of your beloved, to experience giving your love, and receiving another's love, to see the beauty of the
sky turning hues of blue, purple, coral and red at sunset. See it as an
opportunity to practice staying centered by seeing the miraculous, no
matter what is going on in the world you. See the miracle of the hearts
of people opening in love – and name that experience as a miracle. At
work try remembering that "It's all a playground." When things are
going wrong or getting tense in Life remember, "Oh yeah, I am on the
playground!" See how that thought changes your perspective of what
is going on in your office, your relationships – on the playground of
your Life. It will make you laugh, and help you redefine your choices
of actions. That will certainly make a difference in the way you face
the day!

The seagull's message taught me a new way of perceiving the
world. This is a playground! This perception enables us to take ourselves less seriously. Our "work" on the playground should be what
we enjoy doing most! The playground model maintains our obliga-
tions to others, the "good ways" to share with others, to see that they
are nourished, to play in harmony, not hoarding or bullying, but enjoying the beauty, enrichment, truth and peace that Mother Earth affords
to us all. We are here to play, take care of the Divinity in our playground itself and take care of each other, as the Divine Light of God,

playing on the playground!

I do not invite you to this experience lightly. I have worked many years in hospitals and in hospice. I know that Life gives us moments of rainbows among the clouds; however, the clouds can look greenish purple and threatening. I have seen, for instance, a three month old baby completely blue with blank eyes, darkly staring at the ceiling while an army of doctors and nurses were doing chest compressions trying to get a heartbeat back and putting her onto a Life support system. Fifteen minutes can feel agonizingly long in those instances! Then purple for another 30 minutes, and never recovering the pink of oxygen rich tissue. But, I also have connected in those moments with that baby's Soul and asked her if she wanted to come fully into Life, or was embodied only for those few months as her Lifetime. I asked, "What can I do to help you?" In those kinds of experiences does this *feel* like a playground? As you wrap that Soul in a blanket of Love and listen for her communications of what is going on for her, it becomes that playground type experience when your friend falls off the swing, has the wind knocked out of her and you rush to be with her, brush her off, and help her regain her balance. The key factor to remembering it is a "playground" is the Love. Love emanates the trust that what we see in the physical world is not all there is. We are playing in part in a much larger arena of LIFE – and it is all God.

Created In The Image Of God will help you learn to see your Life as an opportunity of unequaled joy as you begin to play on the playground as the true and Authentic You. You will learn what it is like to truly live – enjoying every juicy moment! This is not a Pollyanna form of philosophy. This is simply returning to the Authentic Soul consciousness which you were so attuned to when you came into the world as a child, "new from God." This is an expansion of your incarnate thinking to become centered upon your Eternal and Authentic Soul emanated from God, the Source of All Life.

This course will not introduce you to a new you, but it will return you to a consciousness of the Soul you have been from the God Source. When you are centered on that Authentic Soul consciousness you will find the civil wars within you dissipate and you become increasingly relaxed, happy to be you and do the things that are truly you. You mostly know yourself as the Incarnate Self of your **human** consciousness. You will begin to experience your Eternal Soul, the Authentic You that has always been. If your Authentic Soul is a pond, this Lifetime and who you are in your Incarnate Self is a ripple upon the surface of the pond. As you become conscious of your deeper Soul you will see the Pond, not just the ripple of this Lifetime. In this you will find freedom from the imposed conformity that doesn't fit your Life and you will live in that freedom of choice without guilt. Most of all you will find a contentment with Life, and be able to make a deep commitment to Life; because it's easy – all you have to do is be you!

This contentment is the Peace humans seek. We chase after it down many roads. Sometimes we think money will ease our mind, or health will ease our suffering, or a relationship with the right person will validate us as lovable. However, it all begins within our own Being. It begins when we reach deep within our Being to go beyond our Self, and find that our Eternal Being, our Authentic Soul is an intrinsic and yet unique part of The Whole. Contentment means whatever our house looks like, our finances, our relationships, there is deep peace – a resting in satisfaction. Contentment has nothing to do with the external, it is wholly the internal. It begins with a quiet joy in expressing your unique Soul and it blooms into an uproarious celebration of Being that is nothing short of the dynamic unfolding of God just being God-Self.

You radiate when you are content. The Glory of God is you – and within all that exists.

If we are to show God our gratitude for Life let us do so by truly living that Life to the fullest here on the playground, and fully be who God is emanating us to be. That is pure joy! Living every juicy, bodacious moment of Life!

Are you ready to start this incredible journey? Before you go on a journey it is always nice to have an itinerary of where you will be going.

In the first chapter of our journey you will expand your consciousness of Being. What does it mean to Be? Sometimes we learn about Being by trying to imagine "not Being." We will use some spiritual experiments and practices to open our understanding further on our own existence of Being.

Also in the first chapter you will be introduced to the concept of your Infinite Value. What makes you a person with Infinite Value?

The second chapter of the journey will take you on an adventure through the Four Worlds. You will use the model of the Four Worlds from the Kabbalah, the mystical traditions of Abraham. You will learn about the Infinite Worlds outside of you and the Infinite Worlds within you in this Finite Lifetime and how those two systems of Worlds integrate. The place of that intersection is where the Authentic Soul enters in dialogue with the Incarnate Self; the connection of the Worlds.

Having arrived at your destination of being able to apply the Four Worlds both external and internal to your own Being, you are ready in the third chapter to travel to an exploration of your Incarnate Self and learn the difference between your Authentic Soul and your Incarnate Self. What is your Authentic Soul? From where does it come? What is it like? What is your Incarnate Self? How do they work together? How do they differ? Why do you have an Incarnate Self? How do you know if you are making a decision in your Life from the limitations of your finite Incarnate Self or your Infinite Authentic Soul? The journal pages in this section will be instrumental in your exploration of both your Authentic Soul and Incarnate Self. You will learn about how you interact between the dimensions within you and beyond you. You will begin to create a portrait of your Self and see how that is an imprint of your Authentic Soul for this Lifetime. As an imprint of the Authentic Soul, your Soul will only emanate the Incarnate Self in this Lifetime that you need to fulfill your destiny. You in this Lifetime are only one little facet of the larger eternal diamond that you are.

Having explored these realms, in the fourth chapter you begin the meditative journeys to experience the worlds within your Incarnate Self. When you are sufficiently centered and grounded you will venture forth into the Infinite Four Worlds of your Authentic Soul, by entering the Crystalline Palace and journey as high as you can go toward The Source of All Life ascending the Ancient Grand Staircase. The meditation will take you to the edge of the abyss, which you cannot cross for it is the abyss that erases all differentiation. You cannot return from there because there would not be a "you" to return. After that unique and unspoken experience you descend from the edge of the abyss, having recovered a renewed consciousness of your own uniqueness of existence. You will know better what it means to Be, and to be more specifically you. You are prepared for the experiences of the meditative journey by the chapters leading to them. Your experience will not be as full and may be unstable if you do not give yourself this preparation, so please have patience, and allow your consciousness to open naturally through the reading and integration of the principles given in all of the chapters.

However long it takes for you to make this journey is your story. It is an individual experience and each person takes a unique pathway in this journey. It's a Lifelong journey. You can revisit these pages time and again in the years to come in your Life and continue to grow with each reading because your Life is a spiral of development, and you will be in a new place as you reread the course. The words will speak to you with fresh revelation for your needs at that time. You will be standing in "new light" with which to understand. Say a prayer inviting the Ruach HaKodesh, the Holy Spirit to lead you in all truth. Measure what you read by the inner knowingness of your heart (not just your mind), and use what serves you. Remember, enlightenment is a Life long experience of "receiving", or as it is called, the Kabbalah.

May your journey be blessed as your feet touch the pathway of the Illumination of your Sacred Authentic Soul, the emanation of God.

Chapter 1

Being

In the beginning the Holy One created the Heavens and the Earth. And the Earth was unformed and void, chaos was on the face of the Deep;
Genesis 1:1, 2

Undifferentiation

Can you imagine what Undifferentiated Being might mean? It means to exist but not outside of or in any way definable from all existence. There is no "you", just existence. Think upon this concept for a moment, "not outside of or in any way definable from all existence." That means that existence has no plurality, it is all one. In the state of undifferentiation there is infinite possibility, yet there is "no one thing". Because there is nothing in the sense of no one thing, there is the potential to become anything! The concept of undifferentiation can be thought of as infinite possibility. The moment we define a thing, or create a thing, then the possibilities become limited. Once it is "this" then it cannot be "that". Infinite possibility contains the possibility of all.

It is also possible to say that by containing "no one thing" that Undifferentiated Being can also antithetically be called "nothingness" for in nothingness is Infinite Possibility.

Can you imagine nothing? Stop reading for a moment and try to hold "nothingness" in your mind.

Do you find it difficult? Did you find your mind kept thinking, despite your efforts to clear or quiet your mind? Even if you saw only darkness that is something. If you had any consciousness at all that is something – and not nothingness! We have difficulty thinking about nothingness because we exist! Even thinking is something, not nothing. There are meditations that are "nothing", emptying your mind. However, if you are meditating, that is still something. I know it sounds like a mind game, but keep this concept about nothingness and Undifferentiated Being in your mind while you consider what Differentiation means.

Differentiation

... and the Spirit of The Holy One fluttered over the face of the waters. And The Holy One said, "Let there be Light." And there was Light. And God saw the Light, that it was good;

Genesis 1:3, 4

Sometimes it helps to understand one thing by comparing it to its opposite side. Try this exercise to help you understand the difference between Undifferentiation and Differentiation.

1. Stare **into** a large, clean, white sheet of paper for a few seconds. It must have a smooth surface and no objects on it.
2. What do you see there?
3. Can you "see" anything?
4. Do your eyes keep trying to shift to an edge or somewhere to get a point of reference?
5. Did you notice that you had no depth perception?

In this exercise you cannot really "see" or distinguish anything. This is very close to the concept of Undifferentiated Being.

Now experiment with the concept of Differentiation.

1. Draw a dot on a piece of paper.

●

All of a sudden everything changes, **something** is there. Now there is a visible point of reference. There is Differentiated Being. We have limited what can be there, because something exists (the dot) taking up that space.

2. Now draw a line on the paper extending from the dot.

━━━━━━━━━━ (emanation)

A line is actually a series of tiny dots so close together that they touch, extending into a line. The dot has "emanated" out dots, creating the line.

3. This is Emanation which creates Differentiation.

Now when you stare at the paper what do you see? You can see the white background and the black line! Now there is contrast, a reference point for your eyes, recognition of shape, and slight depth perception. We have further limited, however, what can exist on this paper.

4. Now extend the line to draw a picture of your favorite fruit. I love bananas!

10. Now when you stare at the paper what do you see? Bananas. You have contrast, a point of reference, recognition of a shape and better depth perception. Now we have even further limited what can exist on this paper. Is there any doubt that you can see the Differentiation? However, there is no longer Infinite Possibility for that space of white. The picture carries unique and distinctive Differentiation from the white on the rest of the paper.

11. Draw another picture of the same fruit that you drew before.

Are they the same or do they carry Differentiation from each other? They cannot be same, for each is unique; each holds a **different place in space**. Even if the second picture is generated by electronically copying and pasting the first picture it is still unique in that it occupies a different space on the paper. The second picture has to hold a different place in space or it is not two. No **two** objects can hold distinction, differentiation and be in the same space. If they are in the same space, they are not two, but one. Even identical twins can not be in the same space for each must stand in its own place. Each of us can be the only one to stand in our place. This speaks to you of your uniqueness in the world. You are the only one who can stand in your place.

This experiment illustrates for you the difference between Undifferentiated Being and Differentiated Being. When you stared into the white paper you could not see any distinctive thing at all. But, once you drew a dot, then you drew a line, then formed the line into a shape you could differentiate more and more until you recognized an object which held meaning to you.

This simple experiment explains the concept of Creation coming from the Divine Light as described in the Kabbalah. Do you remember reading in Genesis that there was the void, chaos and formlessness? This is the Undifferentiated Being, the white paper that had no reference point nor carried recognition. The ancient traditions tell us that all was the Divine Light, God (and yet God was something beyond that we cannot conceive of in words). In order for there to be a new creation God contracted God-Self which is referred to as Tzimtzum, in the Hebrew. God contracted from the center out, creating a spherical void, chaos and formlessness. (Do you suppose this is what we might call a "black hole" in the exploration of our Universe today?) Within this "nothingness" God emanated a point of Light in the center. The Light shone in an Infinite ray in Infinite Directions and as it moved from the first point of Light to a "line", the ray, it began creating Dimensions of Being as it shone. In this emanation is the Infinite Possibility coming into Differentiated Being. In this physical world we see this process mirrored in the star at the center of our Universe, the Sun, raying out light energy in all directions, infinitely. Even on the side of the Sun we do not see (it is away from Earth) it is still raying out light energy. This is by way of example in the physical world, but the Higher Dimensions were created, or rayed out, before this physical Universe.

In each of the created or emanated Higher Dimensions there are created Beings with characteristics that hold true to the energy of that Dimension. Each creature is intrinsic to the Energy or vibrations of that Dimension. The chapter on the Four Worlds will explain in more details this creative process.

In the miraculous process of creating by the Divine Light, Eternal

Beings were and continue to be created and energized. The Higher Dimensions are Infinite and Eternal. The concept of Eternal includes what we think of in this world as past, present and future. Another way of thinking of Eternal is the **Always Now**. Past, that which has happened and future, that which is happening or has not yet happened only applies to this Dimension where time is an intrinsic part of the Creation. In the Eternal Being there is always Now.

Your Authentic Soul is your Eternal Being. It was emanated from the Divine Light of God. You are an emanation of God. As God emanates forth God-Being, we call this force the Life-Force. You can feel this energy of Life-force both within yourself and in others. When you are in love you "feel" so alive – the Life-force is flowing freely. When someone is dying and their Soul is disengaging from their body, the Life-force is lessened more and more. You can feel their very low Life-force.

When we **see** this Life-Force we call it **Light**. God isn't Light, but emanates Light. When we **feel** this Life-force we call it **Love**. Love is God's Life-Force moving. When we are "in love" we feel so alive, because the Life-Force of God is moving through us at a high rate of flow. Light and Love are not God, but the Life-Force emanating off of God, the raying out of Being and existence. This is the dynamic unfolding of God. God is BE and all of Creation is the –ING. Therefore, God is BE-ING. *Selah*, (Hebrew for "Pause and think about this!")

We, as human beings and all of Creation are an intrinsic part of the Holy One, the Creator, the Emanator of Life. The Light, the Love, the Life-Force is still not God, the Creator or Emanator. God is still something beyond that in the Kabbalah. We can only talk about that part of God which we experience in the emanations; that which is emanated.

That which is emanated, emanates forth, and that which is emanated, again emanates forth until we get the concept of being created in the image or likeness of the Emanator. We are created in the likeness of the Emanator. Who does that mean I AM? I AM an emanator of Light and Love, the Life-Force of the original Emanator.

This is quite awesome and powerful! You are awesomely and wondrously made! You are an emanation of God. God, The Source is BE, and creation is the "ING" of God. BE is the Emanator, the Undifferentiated, and ING is the emanated, the Differentiated.

Source of All - **BE** All that is emanated - **ING**

BE-ING

God is BE and we (creation) are the ING-ING of God. Say this out loud to hear what I mean by this.

This shows the intrinsic importance of Creation to the Source. BEING can't exist without the ING. That's the emanation. There is God, and there is us, the ING-ING, the intrinsic part of BEING – and it is all God. It is all one word. The Emanator cannot be an Emanator without the Emanation. Separation is an illusion. In the concept of BEING, the ING cannot exist without BE, and vice versa, BE cannot exist without ING. We are ONE. While maintaining multiplicity, duality dissolves. The ONE and the MANY are The One. Selah!

Whenever you are feeling isolated or lonely, meditate on the intrinsic oneness of BEING – it will bring a profound change in your well-being.

Consider a weaver sitting at her loom. Without the cloth can the weaver be a weaver? Is a poet a poet without a poem? The Emanation is intrinsic to the Emanator. The illusion of duality is necessary to this physical world just enough for me to be writing these words to you on this page. We must face one another in order to be in dialogue. But, we can move our consciousness to a higher level of understanding "oneness" in order to treat one another as one, honoring the Divine which is emanating us both at any given moment of time in this Dimension. Our Life-force is the same; we are "made up" of the same. In fact, every tree, mountain, river, ocean, lion, elephant, cat and dog, all of creation is One. What we do affects all of creation, for we are all one in The One. The Emanator and the Emanation, is all Divine.

Adam, the first human being, was created in the likeness or image of God. As God emanated out that which could be face to face with God, then Adam, too, was compelled to have the face to face experience. But it had to emanate from within him. The Kabbalah tells us that Adam was created both male and female, one unit. It continues to tell us that God moved the female part from within to outside of Adam, that Adam may face Eve, "his" female part (by now all that is left within him is the male part). The Kabbalah tells us it is like Siamese twins that are separated. Now Adam has an emanation from within to face and to dialogue with in Life. They are intrinsic to one another, they are mirrors and parables to one another. The first sacred way they are commanded is Peru urvu, "bear fruit and multiply". In the likeness of God they are to emanate new Life. That is to continue the duality to face one another and so on and so on generation to generation. The duality enables dialogue. And the dialogue becomes one. It brings together all that is in one and all that is in the other and creates a new one. That is the ING-ING of God. It is all God. It is all BE-ING. This is the *sod*, the "secret" of Genesis, written in symbolic language. You are wondrously and awesomely made! You may feel like you are having an "awakening" as you open to these concepts. You are "looking" through the eyes of your Authentic Soul, (Eternal Being) and your Authentic Soul is looking through your incarnate eyes. And your incarnate eyes are opening to the consciousness of the Authentic Soul and the realms that are beyond.

This incredible concept means that you have every thing you need within you to deal with Life – and to continue to emanate Life.

How does that work? Let's consider the element of water. Water is made up of H_2O. Water is two molecules of hydrogen to one molecule of oxygen, H_2O. That is what makes it water. If you consider one tiny droplet of water; it is its own little unique droplet, it is H_2O. Or if you consider an entire ocean, take it down to its basic element it is still H_2O. So it is with you as an emanation of God!

You are an emanation of God, The Infinite. That means you are made up of the emanated Life-Force of The Infinite. The energy that God emanates, formed and shaped is you. God is Infinite. That which is emanated from the Infinite is a fraction of Infinity. Any fraction of Infinity is still Infinity! That is you! Everything you need to deal with Life is within you. But how do we call forth that which we desire from within us? How do we access them? It is like having a program on a computer. It is there, but you can't use it until you understand how to access it or call it forth. *The processes of Life teach you how to access the Infinite within you.*

Your Authentic Soul, that energy that has been emanated but exists in the Higher Dimensions outside of time and space in like manner emanates out the Life-force in the energy of a Lifetime in this physical world, in time and space. This is your Incarnate Self, who you are in this Lifetime. Throughout your Lifetime you (your Incarnate Self) has opportunities to learn how to access the Eternal within you, the

Authentic Soul on the Higher Dimensions which is intrinsically emanating your Incarnate Self for specific purposes, your destiny. You have a treasure in the riches of this vast resource from the Higher Dimensions that are accessed from within you!

You may not know how, but you will learn how as you open your willingness to imagine it. Your imagination is a tool for transcendence to the Higher Dimensions. It allows you to put an image to that which is energy and has no physical form. The ability to envision or imagine will be explored in the meditations in Chapter Four. Ultimately, your answers are found within you as you go within your Incarnate Self to transcend to beyond your Incarnate Self. You are best helped to find those answers when another person helps you look within to find what answers resonate with your Authentic Soul. This is the basis of Kabbalistic counseling. The "Rebbe" helps you "see" within your own Self what your Soul is telling you.

Consider the rainbow as another illustration of the oneness of the Emanator and the emanated, the Undifferentiated and the Differentiation. Light from the sun is simply "white light". We can't actually see sunlight itself with our eyes, we just see it reflected off of objects. However, have you ever taken a prism outside when you were a child to "make rainbows"? As the sunlight passes through the prism, the angles of the prism "split" the light into different light waves, displaying the beautiful colors of the rainbow. While we do not see the light, when we pass it through a prism we see all the colors of the rainbow, each its own vibrational energy, a unique light wave reflecting its own color. This illustrates the emanation process of The One and The Many. The Infinite Source contains all, but It is invisible to discern. Then it becomes "split apart" in differentiation and The Many show their uniqueness. Each Dimension and all it contains is like a different color of the rainbow. Each has its own vibrational energy which "looks" different and "feels" different. Orange "feels" different in energy from violet or green. The Life-Force creating each color is vibrating at a different level. Some vibrational levels match or harmonize with your own. Those are colors you like. Others do not, and those are colors you tend not to like. It is hard to be depressed around the color yellow, because when we are depressed we match with "blue" and call it "feeling blue". Yellow is the wrong energy for the "blues" because it has all this effervescence going on; high vibrational energy. Blue is cooler, calmer. The colors are each unique, and can be vastly different, yet, in the rainbow when the colors come together there is a seamless harmony which creates a whole. Taken altogether the rainbow in its multi-colored facets is still All One; it is still the White Light. Selah! Pause and reflect upon this! You are as one of the colors of the Rainbow of Life. You are only one facet, and yet you are intrinsic to the whole. You are of Infinite Value in your existence in the rainbow. Differentiation begins with Emanation.

Infinite Value

And the Holy One said, "Let us make Adam in our likeness
and as is our form;
Genesis 1:26

To consider your own Infinite Value it is necessary to understand the concept of your incarnation in this Lifetime. In the creation story in Genesis we are told that humans are created in the image of God. If we consider that the Holy One is the Emanator, then we too emanate, that is our nature in the likeness of God. Your Eternal Being, which I call your Authentic Soul (indicating your unique differentiation), has been emanated from The Source of All Life. In the likeness of the Source of All Life, your Authentic Soul emanates. And that which it emanates is a finite Lifetime in this finite dimension of the physical world. To be incarnate means that your Eternal Soul, your Authentic Soul in the Higher Dimensions, emanates Life coming into this Dimension of physical being. The Life-force creates as it goes forth from God and your Authentic Soul is part of that Creation. Then, your Authentic Soul, in the "image of God" continues the emanation process, and becomes incarnate, a human being with personality, character, and a destiny for your Life; this is your Incarnate Self. This means that your Authentic Soul, (Eternal Spirit) emanates your Incarnate Self (physical), and you are God's Love made manifest in this Dimension. That's right. You are God's Love made manifest in physical being. That is who you are. Selah.

I am explaining and developing the same basic concepts in several ways, and saying some of the same things over and over because they are big concepts to wrap your mind around. Once you begin to get it intellectually, however, there is an enormous process of getting it down into your emotions. That is another level and that is the level of power! Your emotions are your power plant. Once you really feel in your heart the awesomeness of your existence as Infinite Value, and that you are God's love made manifest your whole Life and perspective on Life changes. It is worth hearing over and over until you "get it" down in your deepest and most sacred part of your Self. Then, you not only see the Divine within your Self, but in other people. You can never look at another human being without respect to the Divine Spark, the Divine in them. When you truly have this you will see the Divine in each pair of eyes you look into from now on throughout your Life. You will also see the Divine within everything that exists, in all Creation. The Divine Energy of the Holy One is in every tree, flower, mountain and river. It is all the living, breathing, Love emanating from God. It is we, and we are one; we are One.

An attribute of God is that God is Infinite. That is Infinite Value! You are an emanation of God. As the Kabbalah says, "Each of us has a spark of the Divine with us". You are a fraction of the Infinite One. If God is Infinite Value, then any fraction of Infinity is still Infinity! You, in your very existence as an emanation of God have Infinite Value. You have everything you need within you to deal with Life. Selah! Pause and think about that for a moment. Go back and read this last paragraph again and again until you get this message deep down. You are Infinite Value, you are God's Love made manifest in the world. Write that on a beautiful piece of paper, and put it on your refrigerator door, put it on your bathroom mirror, put it next to your bed so that it is the last thing you see when you close your eyes at night, and the first thing you see when you awaken in the morning! You are Infinite Value, you are God's Love made manifest in the world.

Infinite Value Exercise

Draw a circle on the left side of the space below:

- This is your Circle of Being. Label it with the word "Being" inside.
- Now draw lines extending out from the right side of your Circle of Being.
- Label each of these lines with something you enjoy doing. These

lines represent expressions of your Self.

- Draw another Circle of Being (representing others) on the right side of the space.

- Sometimes the lines from your Circle of Being are received by the second Circle and other times they are not. When they are received there is a unity between the two Circles. When they are not received there is a void between them. Sometimes other people connect with your gifts and sometimes they do not.

- You may feel devalued when an expression of yourself is not received by others. This can occur especially in the work place or when you are sharing yourself with a loved one. However, you cannot be devalued by the rejection of your expression, the lines coming from your Circle of Being, nor can you be validated by the acceptance of these expressions emanating from your Being. This is because Your Infinite Value is in your **Being**, not your **Doing** the expressions of your self.

- Write "Infinite Value" in your Circle of Being. As you see, nothing outside of that circle can validate or devalue you. You are of Infinite Value in your Being; simply by the fact that you exist.

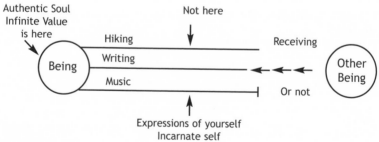

Illustration 1

Your Infinite Value is in the circle of Being, not in the expressions of your Self. If someone does not connect with your expression you are not devalued; it does not have anything to do with your Infinite Value which is in the miracle that you exist.

Sometimes others, (represented by the circle on the right) connect with our lines of self expression. Sometimes they don't. Maybe you love to cook. You spend time (and quite a bit of money) at the grocers picking out all the right ingredients. Then you enjoy preparing the food, cooking, baking and setting the table appropriately for the menu. During the hours of preparation your anticipation is building for how enjoyable this meal will be for all who will share it. When you sit down to the meal you are presenting a gift of yourself to others. If they enjoy it and express their pleasure you have a wonderful feeling of satisfaction. There is a unity and well-being within you. But what if they express their distaste for it – what if they really don't like it? It is like saying, "To hell with your gift, I don't want it." Then how do you feel? Does it feel like you have been devalued? There is a feeling of aloneness and separation. When the gift of an expression of our Self is accepted the principle of the Oneness of All Life is confirmed. When our gift is rejected the rejection belies the principle of Oneness. When others accept our gift (or we theirs) there is a sense of oneness, shared in the expression. This confirms the oneness and connected-ness of the Life-Force, and the truth that we are all emanated from The One Source. We are One. When they do not connect there is a sense of rejection or denial of our oneness. We often feel devalued when these expressions of our Being are not received. It is easy to feel we are of less value. But are we? Where is your Infinite Value? Is it in the lines extending from the circle of your Being? Those lines only repre-sent the expressions of your Being, they are not your Being.

The truth is that our value is not in these expressions of our Being, but in our Being itself. The value is not in the lines of the exercise above, but in our Circle of Being. When the expression of our Self is not received that cannot touch our Infinite Value. Received or not, our Infinite Value is not changed. What ever we experience in Life does not lessen our Infinite Value; we remain Infinite in our Value. Take a moment to reflect on the most difficult times of your Life. They could be times of divorce, financial struggles, the death of a loved one, a failure in school or the work place, even if you are targeted for sexual abuse. I want to tell you that even though you may be targeted, you are only a victim when you name yourself so. That is where **you** have the choice. In each situation remember to say out loud "After _____ happened I still have Infinite Value. I still have all of Me." Say this a few times out loud until the ears of your heart truly hear it. It is powerful. Say it several times a day, each time you begin to feel negative about yourself if you need to. You have everything you need within you to move forward in your Life. Stop and give yourself a few moments with this.

It can be difficult to separate the rejection of our expression of Self from a sense of being devalued in our Infinite Value. This is especially true with our work, what we do to give love and the deepest parts of ourselves that we share. But, again, the truth is that our Infinite Value lies in the fact of our Being, not in what we do or what happens in our lives. I am repeating this principle in many ways because understanding it is so intrinsic to our sense of Infinite Value and ultimately our sense of well-being. You are Infinite Value, always.

To understand your Infinite Value another way, consider a newborn. Have you ever been around a newborn baby? Maybe you have had a child of your own. Do you remember looking at him or her in the crib as a newborn? What did you feel inside? Deep feelings of love well up. Even when we hold a newborn kitten or puppy, how the love overflows from our hearts! And yet, what can this newborn do for itself? A newborn cannot change itself, feed itself, speak in words to you, or even turn over by itself at first. Do you remember the first time you came into the room, looked into the bassinet and realized he or she had turned over on their own? In that moment it is a wondrous feat! A newborn cannot do anything yet. And yet, how could you love it more? It is precious. That newborn's Infinite Value is in the fact of its Being that it exists, not in what it can do or can produce. A newborn, whether it is a child, a puppy or kitten, touches our hearts in tender love by its mere existence! It brings its Infinite Value into our lives by its existence. That is Infinite Value!

Your Infinite Value is your existence, not what you do.

As you grew up you were given messages by parents, teachers, friends and our society of what you are to do or produce to be "accepted" which is often translated and confused with being valued, even loved. The world (especially the advertising world) tells you that to be a valued member of society you must hold certain status by what you do, what you own, who you know, and how you look. That last one is certainly a loaded one! How often from a very early stage did the message come through to you that you must look a certain way to be "lovely" and therefore valuable! Where do you work? Oh you own your own business? How's business (how much money do you make)? You own your own home? Where do you live? You drive a "Roller" (Rolls Royce)? What year? You have children? What do they do? You're single? Have you been divorced? Oh, you are married! How long? Oh, you went to college! Where'd you go? You lived in

England? How long? You stay at home with you're your kids? What does your husband do? How nice, your husband took you out to dinner last night! Where'd he take you? The unspoken judgments are deafening! Leaves you breathless, and every question is loaded with the potential that you will be cubby holed and valued (or de-valued) according to your answer. Phew!

Have you ever lived in a country that places the focus on social interaction – visiting each other? People are always inviting friends over for meals or just spending the evening together? Why don't we? I can just hear the answer – not when I have to get up to work in the morning! I can't have people over, my house is a mess. I don't have nice enough furniture. There isn't room for guests. In those statements work, furniture and house keeping skills have all been placed before people!

Yet, as an adult, think back on the people who have been the most important to you throughout your Lifetime. Think of those who have had the most positive impact on your Life. Does it matter how they looked, where you were, how the room was decorated? What was the most important thing? That they <u>existed</u> in your Life! Most important was the interaction they had with you. You have Infinite Value because you exist; you are Love, God's Love in physical form. **You don't need to learn how to love your Self, you are Love.** Just surrender to the Love that you already have flowing within you and share it with others!

What happens inside of you when you have been working on a project at work, you may have put many hours into it and your supervisor says it isn't good enough and says to start over? Do **you** feel "not good enough?" Does something inside of you feel very angry? It is very difficult to keep our work separate from our selves. The project just didn't fit the situation. It is not a devaluation of you. The work is an expression of you, true, but it is not you. You are the Circle of Being you drew. Your Infinite Value lies in that existence. The anger rises in us when our Incarnate Self mind accepts the idea that we are "not good enough" by what we have produced, because our Authentic Soul knows we are of Infinite Value. An adult who has been abused as a child (in any of a myriad of ways) often grows up to be an adult with deep underlying anger. Why? Because back when the child was being abused his or her Authentic Soul (Eternal Being in the Higher Dimensions) knows the truth and unconsciously says "I didn't deserve to be thrown through that plate glass window. I am a Being of Infinite Value" and it cries. The Incarnate Self gets angry as a defense mechanism, defending something very precious to the person, their Infinite Value. We each deserve to be treated as divine emanations of God with Infinite Value. When we see it in our Self, then we recognize it in others.

Have you ever been through a divorce? Oy! You just think you are beginning to heal from the hurt and disappointment and then you hear "your song" on the radio, or you are filling out forms in your doctor's office and for the first time have to check off "divorced" under marital status. In those moments when the pain is fresh your Being feels quite devalued. But this is a matter of focusing your Self (Incarnate mind) on your Authentic Soul, the reality of you Infinite Value, no matter what. Your Authentic Soul is still whole; you realize you have lost nothing of your Self. However, we live in a world that tells us otherwise, and it is easy to become focused on the imposed conformity of the society around us that tells us something is wrong with us for having "divorced" checked on the form of our Life. This imposed conformity trap begins in our childhood.

As adults who are striving to reach balance in our lives we examine the messages our parents gave us in their words and their actions. We can recognize that some of the messages serve us in our lives and others do not. Some of the messages our parents gave us were about their "stuff" rather than wisdoms for Life. We then, are empowered by our choice to let go of the messages that do not empower us, for those very same messages deny our Infinite Value. Our Infinite Value is not affected by what we do or don't do. It is and will be as long as we exist.

Nothing from outside the circle you labeled Being can affect your Infinite Value, it is in your Being. The only place you are devalued in any way is in the cloud of your own mind. That mental cloud blocks the Light that you are. It does not mean you are devalued; it is merely a cloud blocking the Light. You are standing in the shadows of your own cloud. You are still Infinite Value even in your own denial of it.

To learn how to process and release the clouds blocking the Light of your Infinite Value turn to the Journal Pages and try exercise # 5, "Messages of Infinite Value". It will bring an insight as to how you began thinking of yourself as less than Infinite Value, and what to do to feel your Infinite Value.

The Kabbalah says that if God were to blink for a moment all of creation, (including you and me) would disappear! You are the constant emanation of God. No one else can fill your place in Creation. God breathes out the breath of Life – and you breathe it in. As you breathe out you return the breath of Life back to God. This is the dance of Life. Dance with all your heart!

You can picture Creation as a huge puzzle, and each of us is a puzzle piece. Each piece has a specific shape and size that fits together with others around it; and when you get them all connected in place what do you have? It is a picture that is the sum of its parts and shows clearly what it is only when all the parts are together. The puzzle of Creation is not complete without your puzzle piece in this moment of time in this Dimension. Is any one piece the picture? No, but without each piece the picture is not whole. Without you there would be a hole left in the picture of the puzzle. With you it is whole. Add to this incredible concept that you are an Authentic Soul that's an Eternal Being raying out your Incarnate Self who in this Lifetime at this moment of time in history! This is a historic moment in history because you are uniquely who you are in this Lifetime – and you will never be this person again. Even in the event of living other Lifetimes, you are who you are at this time only for this time. You have never been in our world before as who you now are and will never be again.

I want you to write your name in the sentence below and read it out loud. Read it as many times as it takes for you to not only know this with your intellect, but to feel it in your heart:

There has never been a _____ in the world before, and there will never be again. This is a unique time in the history of the world; I AM here.

Read it again! Wow! That is you. This is a unique time in the history of our world for your Being here. That is your Infinite Value. You are a differentiated emanation of God with Infinite Value. You have an Authentic Soul and you have incarnated into the human form, your Incarnate Self, in this world for a purpose and with reason. You have everything you need within you. You are given help from others who hold their own place as puzzle pieces, (humans, animals, nature beings and beings of other Dimensions). They help you call forth your inner resources through shared experiences. And you help them by being in their lives to be the Creation God has emanated them to be.

There was a story circulated on the internet about a man who was walking along the beach. The tide had gone out suddenly and very violently, stranding starfish and sea creatures along the shoreline. The man was bending down, picking one up, and throwing it back out into the water. Eventually, another man walked up and said what are you doing? The man said, "I am throwing these starfish back out into the ocean, so they will live." The man said, "Look along the beach, how many there are! Imagine along the entire coastline how many there are! How could what you are doing make any difference? The old man bent down, picked up another starfish, tossed it out into the waves and said, "Made a difference to that one." You make a difference because you are here. You make a difference to each person around you, who you have met and those you have yet to meet. Everything you do in the world is connected to others, just like the puzzle pieces. By an act as seemingly insignificant to some as throwing a starfish back into the ocean, to the starfish it is Life and death. Your Life carries meaning. Everything we do creates a vibrational energy that goes out into the world and affects the vibrations of others and of the whole. What power! What responsibility! What grace! Even our words are vibrations that carry effect by content and energy. My Rabbi says his father used to say that someday a machine will be invented that can read the vibrations that are recorded in the walls by the words and actions of those in the room. They will then be able to tell everything that has ever happened there. We are vibrational energy, and affect the world around us through what we emit in our actions and words. If our vibrations could be recorded on a wall, imagine the effect on others. What a beautiful plan Creation is; that each of us is Infinite Value, and has all we need within us to deal with Life, and yet we need one another to bring forth that strength from within us!

If you are Infinite Value and have everything you need within you, then why do we need each other? Why do we need community? Let's take an example of Infinite Value in community with the model of the Sun.

The Sun rays out light in all directions – even the side which is away from the Earth, which we don't see is still raying out sun-light. Each ray of light is a fraction of the light sent out by the Sun. Any fraction of light is still light. God, the Infinite is raying out Infinity and any fraction of Infinity is still Infinity. We have Infinity within us. We have established that previously. However, even though we have this Infinity within us we do not always know how to access all that is within us. This is where we need others. Other people help us to access that which is within us, which we do not even see within ourselves. How does that work?

Have you ever had a friend or partner who felt they just could not do an enormous task before them, but you knew they could? You encourage them and give them the gift of your faith in them. But are you really "giving" them faith? You cannot apply faith to someone else from the outside. Actually, you are calling forth the faith that is within them already. Your faith calls forth their faith. Step by step they accomplish the impossible task they set out to do. So we call forth from within one another what we cannot see in our selves. Father Cornelius van der Poel calls this "being a co-creator with God" for we have helped that person be who God created them to be from the beginning.

When we have an ongoing relationship, then in turn our partner, husband, wife, calls forth from within us that which we cannot see within ourselves and helps us become who we are. In your intimate relationships in Life you are never the same after knowing that person as you were before you met. They have helped you become who you are now; and you have helped them become who they are now. In that you can never be separated; as long as you exist you will be part of one another in that way. Even if your loved one dies, you are together in this, you are who you are because of them, they are who they are because of you. We need each other to become fully who we can be.

Can a "born teacher" teach without students? Don't the brightest students and the most difficult students challenge the teacher to find ways to awaken them to the subject? If this is true on a one to one basis, then how much more so is it true in community? Learning to maintain peace within community calls forth our sense of balance between the expression of our individual development and the communal needs. Addressing the needs of society and our community calls forth the highest within us in the multiplicity of our individual gifts. The process of shifting our world into Enlightenment (or bringing the Messiah or Messianic Age) we must individually and collectively have a paradigm shift of acknowledging the Infinite Value within our Self and recognizing and honoring the Infinite Value in one another – and all Creation; for this is all an emanation of the Creator. It is all God. Selah.

Just imagine what Life would be like for you if you had been taught this about yourself from the time you were an infant! What are some of the issues you struggle with in Life that would not be issues for you today? Teach your children and grandchildren about their Infinite Value and watch how they bloom!

After experiencing the "moment of awe" of realizing your own

Being as an emanation of God there comes the feeling of loving to be you, accepting all parts of you, and embracing the gifts you offer to the Whole. You truly enjoy being you and you are able to open to the love already flowing within you. There is a new aspect to the wonderful experience of love in your Life. You are able to truly honor your Being.

That flow of love in your Life is eternally there. When you love someone, you love that person's Being, not just their actions. Some actions you like and some you don't like, but you still love the person. So it is with your own Incarnate Self and Authentic Soul. Do you love your *Being* or your *actions*? Actions are based on choice. At any point in time you can make a choice and in the next moment of "now" you are free to choose again. Those are your actions, your expressions; but, your Being (the circle in the exercise above) is the steady keel of your ship through the waters of many choices. Just imagine the joy of awakening in the morning and thinking, "I love being me!" The love that is flowing through you is your existence, it is in your Being and nothing you do or do not do can change it. It is eternally there as long as you exist! You are eternally Love. Selah!

And now with what you know, you will never be the same.

Before moving on to the next chapter on the Four Worlds, take a moment to fill in the following Journal Pages with your own thoughts, feelings and truths. Remember, there are no "right or wrong" answers. The answers are the way you understand yourself at this time. You might like to date these pages and re-visit them from time to time. As time goes on you will see your own spiritual journey in your answers.

Journal Pages

1. Give an example of Undifferentiated Being in your Life.

2. What does emanation mean?

3. Name one thing that you emanate or have emanated.

3. What does it mean for you to be a Differentiated Being?

4. Experiencing joy in your own Being involves letting go of some of your "shoulds".

A. List some of the "shoulds" that **you** think you **should** fulfill:

B. Now list "shoulds" that <u>others</u> have told you that you <u>should</u> fulfill:

C. How many of the "shoulds" in A. actually come from B.?

D. Now list the "shoulds" that you see as **inauthentic** to who you are, and intend to release them. (Most of these will come from C.)

E. Now list the "shoulds" that you enjoy fulfilling in your Life and which you set an intention to keep.

Meditation

Releasing the inauthentic "Shoulds"

This is a meditative exercise to help you release the "shoulds" and unhealthful expectations of yourself. As you do this meditation you are also exercising your trust in God and the Angels to care for you and to intervene in your Life for good. This meditation will become a spiritual tool for you to use from now on throughout your Life.

First choose a "should" from your D. list.

Sit comfortably, take three deep breaths. As you exhale follow your breath upward.

Open the sacred space (called Keter or Crown) which is about 6 inches above the top of your head.

With each breath move your focus of energy through that opening, through the portals of the Dimensions, toward the Source of Your Divine White Light.

Cup your hands, and picture holding your "should" **that you are releasing** in your cupped hands.

Raising your cupped hands, lift this "should" up to the Divine Light of The Holy One.

Ask the Holy One and the Angels to take it for you and to give you enlightened wisdom about it.

Part your hands and allow that "should" to fall through your hands, turning it over into God's care. The Angels will take it for you.

Watch to see where it goes and what happens to it as God and the Angels receive it.

Listen quietly for any wisdom that God or the Angels speak to your heart.

Now that is emptied out of you. It is no longer part of your Being.

Take a deep breath and exhale. Your breath is your spiritual seal that you put on your intention as you send it out into the Universe, up to the Heavens.

Repeat this process with each "should" you or others impose upon you that is **not** authentically you.

After the last "should" has been set free take a deep breath of freedom! You are free of the imposed conformity you have set upon yourself. You are free to be authentically you.

When you feel complete come back to this time and place, this room and all that is present around you.

Take a moment to record what happened with each of the "shoulds" as you released it to the Angels. Record the wisdom you were given about the "should".

Note: You may want to take a few days to do this exercise individually with each of the "shoulds". They do not need to be released all at once. Be sure to drink plenty of clear water whenever you are doing meditations that are clearing you of those things which inhibit your Life. Now you have this meditation to use for the rest of your Life as a spiritual tool to clear your Life of anything that no longer serves you and to release that which you no longer desire to hold in Life. You can put this tool in your spiritual tool box and use it wisely and often!

5. Messages of Infinite Value

A. Think of and write down a message that your parents gave you about yourself that does not serve you in Life.

Example: "Children should be seen and not heard."

B. How has that message negatively affected your Life?

C. Does that message carry with it the message that you are of Infinite Value simply in your Being?

D. You can let go of that message by saying out loud, Truth that refutes the message and confirms your own Infinite Value.

Message of Truth:

Confirmation of your own Infinite Value:

Example:

Message of truth: Each child is an emanation of God in the world.

To see and hear a child is to see and hear the Divine expression. Each child carries Infinite Value in his or her mere existence.

Confirmation of your own Infinite Value: I am an emanation of God; even when I was a child, I carried Infinite Value.

Try this with each of the messages that you received as a child that do not serve you and release them from your Life. You may need to say your Message of Truth and Confirmation message out loud many times a day at first in order to get it to move from your intellectual understanding down into your heart. When it is deeply seated in your heart, your will feel your Infinite Value!

6. Write a few paragraphs about your Infinite Value. What is it? What does it mean to you? How does it impact your Life? How does knowing that you are Infinite Value, God's love made manifest in physical form change your Life?

Notes

Chapter 2

Four Worlds

Introduction

The Four Worlds of Creation is a concept from the theoretical Kabbalah. Even though these concepts have been handed down and received for thousands of years you will find that they are metaphysical in language and still speak to our scientific exploration of the Universe today.

The physical world in which we live, work, and play is actually part of a vast, complex system of interrelated worlds or Dimensions. Each Dimension is Infinite, unique and has an effect on the physical world we know. Our world has its influence upon these other worlds as well. Each of these worlds reflects and illumines its Light on the world "below" it, projecting itself upon the next. We use the word "below" not as in spatial relation, but in relationship to its development from The Source and also therefore in its transparency of Light; for the "higher" the World, the brighter and more transparent its Light, its Energy. Each world has its modifications, it purposes, its created beings and its ability to interpenetrate both up and down in the Worlds or Dimensions.

The mystical language of the Prophet Isaiah gives us the key words that are used for the Four Worlds, Infinite Dimensions and Finite.

For so says the Holy *One* of *Emanation*, Who *created* the Heavens, and *formed* the Earth, and *made* it;

Isaiah 45:18

The Four Worlds are Emanated, Created, Formed and Made. We see this concept implanted within this statement from the Holy One. As you read about each of the Four Worlds you will explore the meanings and differences of the processes at work in the Universe, created, formed and made. They are integrated and inseparable in existence.

To understand the development of the Worlds of the Kabbalah we must venture back in time and space to a place that is not and a time before Time. Sound interesting? Here we go.

Ayin, Ain Sof, V'Ain Sof Or
Nothingness, Infinite Possibility, and Endless Light

The concept of the Four Worlds is based upon the Infinite and Eternal. However, to speak about the Infinite we must use words which are finite. So you can see the place to overcome the problem of spatiality is in our thinking. As creatures in a physical world we are very time and space oriented, however, to speak of the Infinite and Eternal we must transcend time and space and put our brains out on a stem, so to speak, to imagine elements beyond our physical world experience.

Can you imagine what it was like before Creation? Imagine there being nothing, no Being at all. Nothingness. We have a hard time putting this through the computer in our heads because the moment you try to think of nothingness, there is something, so it is not nothingness! The ancient ones named this difficult concept *Ayin* which means "nothing, there is not." This is what we know as God before there was .... Within Ayin is everything that can be – Infinite Possibility; and only in nothingness is there Infinite Possibility. Once something is manifest, there is limitation and there is no longer Infinite Possibility. Take some time to think about this concept:

Nothingness, within which there is Infinite Possibility.

This Infinite Possibility was named *Ain Sof,* which means "Without End." So there is Ayin, nothingness, within which is Ain Sof, that which is without end.

The Ain Sof is Undifferentiated Being; it is All Light. For there to be Differentiation, the emanation or radiation of Light must take place. However, there was no "place" Creation (Differentiation) to exist, because the Ain Sof is all. In order for there to be anything differentiated from the All Light there had to be a space for Creation to exist! This space was opened by an event called *Tzimtzum,* or the contraction of God. This contraction was a pulling in or back of the Ain Sof, Without End. The Energy of All Being "pulled back" or contracted creating a "space" which was spherical reaching toward all directions, infinitely. Remember, we are trying to express esoteric concepts of Energy movement and transformation with finite words, so we can only approximate the description, allowing our words to be a springboard for our Soul to "remember". This concept is an attempt to express with human understanding that which is previous to human existence, and yet human existence was in God the Emanator even before the emanation! We are reaching beyond human experience to conceive of our *potential* of existence within God.

God contracted the Light from a point at the "center" moving outward in every direction which created a spherical space. The Light pulled back in all directions creating Dark space. It is like a Black Hole in our now existing Universe. The Light is what is contracted.

There is always something in nature to help us understand the transcendent concepts of Creation. The eye is a powerful illustration of Tzimtzum. Consider the iris, the muscle tissue that gives the eye its color. When the light is very dim, and the optical nerves need more light to enter to distinguish objects, so the iris receives the signal from the brain to contract. As the iris contracts what happens to the pupil, the dark area in the middle of the eye? It seems to expand. I say "seems" because the pupil is actually just the opening of the eye, an empty space allowing more light to enter the inner eye. This is the action of Tzimtzum, the contraction of Ain Sof, contracting and making space, as an iris contracts and creates a space, the pupil, the opening of the eye.

"Eye of God"

Helix Nebula – NBC 7293

Hubble Space Telescope – Advanced Camera for Surveys. NOAO 0.9m – Mosaic 1 Camera

NASA, NOAO, ESA, The Hubble Helix Team, M. Meixner (STScl), and T.A. Rector (NRAO), STScl-PRC03-11a

The Hubble telescope has given us incredible pictures of a nebula that has been named the "Eye of God" which illustrates in nature this concept. In the space created by Tzimtzum, the contraction of God, Creation took place.

It was as if God breathed in so that God could breath out and the breathing out was the beginning of Creation, the emanation of God, which became the heartbeat of the Universes.

Before you can breathe out what must you do? Breathe in! Tzimtzum. The muscles of your rib cage contract which pulls your lungs out, creating more space within the cells of the lungs to pull in oxygen. What is the first thing a baby does when it comes into this world? If you answered "Cry" you are in the top 95% of people I have asked this. No! The point of getting a baby to cry is to get him or her to take a breath! To cry you must **first** breathe in air! What is the last thing a person does as the Soul transcends the body and leaves this Dimension? We breathe out. Thus, in the image of God, we contract first and then we exhale.

This process of breathing in and then exhaling is the completion of God's power name **YHVH** the Tetragrammaton that is the ineffable name of God. Some people believe that this name for God is not to be pronounced. It was the name the High Priest proclaimed three times from behind the veil of the Holy of Holies on Yom Kippur. The people in the courts would prostrate themselves at the sound of the name. Because it is the ineffable name of God there are those who believe it is never to be spoken, and substitute this power name with a lesser name; and there are even those who say the pronunciation has been forgotten with antiquity. Some try to pronounce the name as Jehovah or Yahweh. However, the Kabbalist invokes this power name with great care and knows that it is ineffable because it is not spoken, it is breathed. It is the very Breath of Life name. The **YH** is the inhale and the **VH** is the exhale. The moment we enter the world as an infant our first act is to begin breathing the powerful name of God; and the last action we take in this world as our Soul transcends the body, is to finish breathing the power name of God as we breathe out our last breath. From birth to death our lives are a string of pearls of breathing in and out, the power name of God, **YH-VH, YH-VH, YH-VH**. Each moment we are proclaiming God's name, Breath of Life. It is not spoken, it is breathed. This is why focusing on your breath is such an effective tool for transcending in meditation. It is the Tzimtzum and creation over and over again – the Breath of Life; creating space and filling it!

When we speak the voice is utilized on the exhale. That is why people who are on a ventilator can only speak when the ventilator is allowing air to move the air out of their lungs. Our voice, sound sets a vibration out into the world, and that vibration creates change. In the image of God, we create with our words which are the vibrations of our breath moving through the body (vocal chords). At first it may only be a cry; but the cry of the newborn moves the world. It begins with the act of Tzimtzum.

Imagine "all Light". Then from a single point the Light is contracted back in all "directions". This would create a sphere of "no Light". But remember, this event is going on **before** Creation. It is into this "sphere" of void that God emanates. The book of Genesis speaks of this event as *tohu v'vohu,* formless chaos and void.

Now the earth was unformed, chaos and void, and Darkness was upon the face of the abyss. And the "Breath of God" (Ruah Elohim) fluttered over the face of the vapors (setting up a vibration as waves of energy).
Genesis 1:2

Notice the earth is mentioned as if it existed, but as you read the words carefully, you see that there is no earth, only unformed chaos and void in a powerful Darkness (absence of Light) in the abyss formed through the Tzimtzum. Then God sets in motion vibrations of Energy – Life-force which causes a rippling effect as on the face of vapors. (The ethers of Creation are inferred as a water metaphor). These opening lines of the book of Genesis illustrate the symbolic language of the mystics describing the Kabbalistic concepts on Creation.

After Tzimtzum comes the emanation of Creation. As the abyss (space) is created the Light begins to spin a thread of Light into the utter Darkness from the vibrations (voice) set in motion by the "flutter" of the Ruach Elohim or Breath of God. They mystical language expresses this as "God said".

And God said, *"Y'hi Or* , Let there be Light," and there was Light.
Genesis 1:3

Remember, this is before the creation of the Heavens or the Earth, the Universe and the planets. This is not referring to the light of the Sun, but the Divine Light of the emanation of Life-force creating the Dimensions.

This emanation was in the form of a single point of Light at first. This is called *Ain Sof Or*. *Or* is the Hebrew word for Light. Ain Sof Or is the Light Without End, or Endless Light. In anthropomorphic terms, God breathed in, Tzimtzum, and then God breathed out again and that was emanation of Creation.

World of Atzilut - Emanation

The Ain Sof Or was at first a point of Light, but just as quickly as it came to be, it began to emanate Light. It began raying out, for this is the nature of Light. What happens when you walk into a dark room with a flashlight? The second you turn on the flashlight the light goes forth into the darkness and illumines everything in its path by "raying out" the energy of light. If there is a dark room and a room filled with light, what happens if you open a door between the rooms? The darkened room becomes light because the light from the light-filled room rays out into the darkness. Does the light-filled room ever become dark from the darkness in the dark room? No! The energy of Light rays out into the darkness, illumining and reflecting Light from all objects. This is the World of *Atzilut*. It is the World of Emanation (of the Light).

Atzilut, means "emanation" for this is the purpose of the Divine Light – to illuminate and to create new dimensions in its path.

Atzilut is pronounced to rhyme with "Got-zi-loot" with the accent on the last syllable. Make this your word by repeating it out loud a few times, Atzilut, Atzilut, The World of Atzilut.

This first of the Four Worlds has the characteristics of Undifferentiated Being emanating as Differentiated Being. Atzilut is an infinite dimension or world, meaning it goes out in all directions to Infinity. The Kabbalists speak of Infinity as the point at which two energies traveling in opposite directions meet. That is the point of Infinity. (Meditating upon this concept is definitely a stretch in the abstract for our finite minds. It can only be approached from outside our finite consciousness, outside of time and space, without proximity or boundary.)

The World of Atzilut is the highest and finest energy of the Four

Worlds. You do not transcend all the way into Atzilut in med
for if you did you would become undifferentiated and there would not
be a "you" to return to your physical body and earth plane consciousness. Having said this, it is also the ultimate destination of all creation
to become increasingly refined in energy, carrying higher and higher
Light to the end that we will all move back into the Oneness of Atzilut
to be emanated once more. This is the heartbeat of God. This is not a
cycle of reincarnation, but is a longer process of Being. The concept
of living our Lifetime on this earthly plane will be explored in the
World of Assiyah, the fourth of the Four Worlds.

Atzilut, the Infinite emanation creates "filters" through which the
Light passes, creating, reflecting, and projecting itself upon the next
of the Four Worlds, the World of *B'riyah*.

World of B'riyah - Created

The result of the emanation or illumination of the Divine Light in
Atzilut is that a new Dimension was created. Imagine the Dawn. As
soon as the Sun peeps over the horizon its rays spread out over the
landscape. Even before the Sun itself appears, the rays of Light pre-
cede it illumining pathways of Light across the canvas of the sky. I
call it "God-Light". So the Ain Sof Or, the point of Light began emanating Light, or raying out the Divine Light into Creation. As the
Light moved forth its vibrations created a new dimension, or World of
B'riyah, which means "Universe or Creation." B'riyah is pronounced
to rhyme with "free-yah" with the accent on the last syllable. Make
B'riyah your word by saying B'riyah out loud: B'riyah, B'riyah,
B'riyah. The created World of B'riyah is the dimension of pure
intellect.

This World of B'riyah is known as the World of Intellect or the power of thought. This is not fact finding or the accumulation of knowledge, but the very power to think – our intellect. This World of Intellect has a very thin energy. Have you ever had a thought and then lost it? It can be quite difficult to retrieve, because the energy is so thin. Have you ever been waiting for a break in a conversation to say something and then when you had an opportunity you could not remember what you were going to say? A thought is thin energy and can be difficult to hold and recall. We often use memory traces to lead us back to the thought. If you remember the last thing said before your thought you can follow the path of energy flow that leads you back to your original thought. Have you ever found yourself in a room saying to yourself, "Now, what did I come in here for?" If you return to the room you were in when you had the thought the thought will often come back to you. It is as if the thought is still hanging in the air. There is a reason for this phenomenon which we will explore in the section on connecting the Four Worlds to the four elements in this physical world.

Have you ever pondered the power of thought? It is a wondrous and awesome power, the power of intellect. This is a dimension that is Infinite and all that exists in it is the power to think, the energy that creates the thought process. The World of B'riyah is outside of time and space. It is not the thoughts themselves, but the POWER of thought.

B'riyah is the first world of differentiation. It is not this physical world of creation yet! From All Being, The One we have moved now to differentiation. No two thoughts exactly alike. Even the power of thought has differentiation in vibrations, intensity, and the Light it is carrying. The Divine Energy moves across into the very high vibrational energy of thought, thus Creating all that is. Before anything exists it is in the World of B'riyah, thought. Thought precedes everything of Creation. But, all that is, does not exist in manifestation within B'riyah, for each World proceeding from the former continues to ray out the Divine Light, or shine forth the Light which moves through "screens" or filters to the next World creating anew as it floods forth. As you can see from the process of going from Atzilut to B'riyah the worlds are inter-dimensional and interlocked. Each projects and reflects onto the next. The Light also travels back up through the Four Worlds. The Four Worlds are One and yet each is different, carrying the Light and Life-force of God in differing degrees and textures.

Have you ever seen Light as a color filter is put across it? It is still Light, but it appears different because the Light waves are restricted further and further and changed in levels. There are high or fast vibrations and low or slow vibrations. They each create anew. Since B'riyah is outside of time and space we are not considering these vibrations as high or low in space, but in flow of power. Do the vibrations have more or less power flowing in them? To visualize this is concept we must bring an abstract concept into physicality as in the illustration below.

Higher vibrational Energy carrying more Light

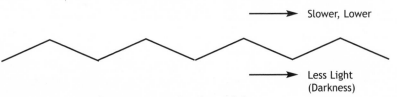

Lower vibrational Energy carrying less Light

Fear and Love as same Continuum

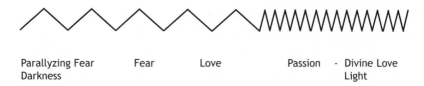

Parallyzing Fear   Fear   Love   Passion - Divine Love
Darkness   Light

Continuum of Fear and Love

The World of B'riyah is the place of random patterns of points of the Divine Light. The term random pattern may seem like an oxymoron, an antithetical term. However, it is referring to the Light coming through in points that are patterned in the Divine Mysteries, but do not seem relevant. Relevance of the points of Light will be introduced in the next Infinite Dimension that is being projected through B'riyah. B'riyah is the place of pattern, seemingly random.

There is a story in the High Holy Day Machzor (Prayer Book) about a little boy who was not educated beyond knowing the Hebrew Aleph-bet (Alphabet), for he worked with his family's flock all day and had no time for further education in the prayers. On Yom Kippur, the great Day of Atonement, he was sitting outside the window of the Synagogue listening to the prayers of the people in the service. He felt very badly that he could not join the people in the prayers. So he whispered a prayer to God saying, "I wish to pray the great prayers of our people, but I am just a shepherd boy and do not know the prayers. I do know all the letters of the Aleph-bet, though, so I am going to recite all the letters to you and I will ask you to put them in the right order for the prayers."

This little one's faith was exemplary of lifting up whatever you have to touch the heart of The Compassionate One. However, this is also an illustration of the Infinite World of B'riyah. The Lights in random pattern are as the letters of the Aleph-bet. They will be put in relationship by Divine Order. We can not understand them, but it is enough to simply hold them; let them be.

When the Light from B'riyah filters down (not in space, but in vibrations) it creates another Dimension called the World of *Yetzirah*, or the World of Formation.

World of Yetzirah - Formation

The word Yetzirah means to form in the way a potter gives clay a form, and a shape. Yetzirah is pronounced Yet-see-rah, with the accent on the last syllable. Say Yetzirah out loud a few times to give yourself a familiarity with its sound.

The World of Yetzirah is a Higher Dimension in the Infinite known as the World of Emotions. Our emotions are what give our thoughts form and shape in the sense of expansion or contraction of energy. Our Love for instance expands us, causes us to move outwardly. Our fear causes us to pull our energy in and shut down. All of the emotions give a pull and texture to our thoughts. The energy of the World of Yetzirah is quite a bit "thicker" in that it is very powerful. It is the power plant Dimension. What has more power than our emotions? Love is the most powerful energy flowing in the Universe.

A thought is just a thought until we attach to it an emotion. It is then that it has the energy and power to come through to the physical world, changing our lives by our actions. Remember that illustration about having a thought and waiting to get into a conversation to express it and not being able to remember what you were going to say by the time it is your turn? That is the thinness of the energy of B'riyah, the World of Thought. However, have you noticed that the more emotion that is attached to that thought you are holding the harder it is to wait for that opening – sometimes resulting in our jumping into the conversation out of turn. We sometimes "step on others' tongues" in our heat of emotion to say what we are invested in saying. We can't even concentrate on what the other person is saying while we are focused on formulating what we are going to say. Our emotions give rise to actions from our thoughts. The "voltage" of a thought is "amped up" by our emotions.

Have you ever had a dream which, upon awakening in the morning, you can't quite remember was about? However, the feelings of the dream are easily accessed. (You can sometimes hold the feelings and then scenes of the dream will re-appear in your thoughts). If you can't remember what you dreamed, you will usually remember the feelings you had in the dream. That is an important key, for remember, Yetzirah indicates the power of your dream. The feelings of the dream can link you to the dream's content, because you are traveling from the World of Yetzirah up to the World of B'riyah.

The World of Yetzirah is the dynamic energy that births our thoughts into action. It is the balanced integration of our emotions that enable us to speak wisely. It is the next step of Being, raying out in the "-ing" resounding through the Dimensions.

It is important to understand our emotions in order for us to rightly use the power of them. Take the emotion of love for example. Most people have felt love for someone or something at some time in their lives. Where does that love come from? It comes from outside of you, but through you. If the object of your love is removed from your presence or even this world, your love remains. It is not coming from the object of your love; it is coming through you from beyond time and space, from the Infinite World of Yetzirah. Understanding that enables you to use your love as a bridge that spans the Dimensions and connects you heart to heart, whether in the presence of your loved one or in their absence. The emotion of love enables the unity of your Souls. This unity is relationship. The World of Yetzirah is the place of relationship. The **random pattern** of B'riyah is put into **relationship** when the energy passes through Yetzirah.

Yetzirah is a Dimension, going out in all directions Infinitely. It is outside of our physical Being. Yetzirah, the Power to Feel, gives to the power of thought form and shape and relationship. Now the Light is ready to project out the next world, and put the related pattern into Action – creating the World of Assiyah, the physical World of Action.

World of Assiyah – Made

The fourth world, the World of Assiyah, is the Dimension of our Universe the physical world. Our scientists tell us that everything in the world is in motion; even the chair you are sitting on is made of molecules vibrating very quickly together to form that object. Everything in this Dimension is in motion. This is the World of Action or the Power of Doing.

When a thought becomes attached to an emotion it has the power to move through the screen that filters the energy and creates the actions around us and within our lives.

What happens when something stops motion in this world? It no longer has the energy to exist in this dimension. But, matter is neither created nor destroyed, it only changes form. Change is motion, it is an action.

Even death is an action. The heart stops, the breath stops, and the Soul leaves the body to move out of this Dimension of physicality. The body follows the same pathway as a tree. When a tree dies it falls to the ground and begins to break down and returns to the elements of the earth. There it continues in "motion" as the ground itself is alive! It provides nutrition for the roots of other living plants.

In the Hebrew traditions it is traditional when a person dies to allow the body to return to the elements of Mother Earth as quickly as possible. It is thought that the Soul is more fully freed from the body as the body returns to Mother Earth from where it came. Metaphysically, the sooner the body completes the transformation from being a human form without the Life of the Soul to returning to the elements of Earth, the sooner the body may continue in the Life of Mother Earth. It is believed that at the time of the Messiah, the Messianic Age when this Dimension shifts to a higher plane, the Earth will yield up the Life of the bodies she cradles in resurrection of the Light Body. Even in this, in the World of Assiyah there is action, always action.

In order for matter to take motion what is necessary? Space! My arm is here, and now I extend it out to there. What was necessary for me to take this action? There has to be space. Every action is locked into space. There is a second factor, though, in this World of Assiyah, and that is time. Time measures action! It takes a certain length of time to complete a day. The time is set by the turning of the Earth on its axis, revolving around the Sun, which we call days and seasons. With the advent of using quartz crystals in our watches we no longer keep time by the sun, but we are now keeping time by the vibrations of the quartz, that is, how many vibrations per second. Vibrations are actions. Time is an artificial overlay created by humanity to enable us to create accuracy for our actions. You and I may *meet* at a certain agreed upon *time*. You *work* for a certain length of *time*. It takes so many *hours* to *travel* from New York City to Boston. How many *hours* did you *sleep* last night? How *long* do you take to *eat* lunch? As you can see, time is relative only to actions. And actions take space to be executed. So time and space are relative to the basis of actions and intrinsic to the World of Assiyah. This is the physical World of Assiyah, the World of Actions. Time and Space do not apply to the Higher Dimensions of Atzilut, B'riyah or Yetzirah. More will be explained on this in the section of the *Three Factors* later in this chapter.

I want to bring in here an understanding of the mystical teaching of Creation of this Universe in Genesis in relationship to the concept of a day. The measure of the turning of the Earth to give a time of darkness and a time of light, however, should not be confused with the Biblical "day" of Genesis 1. The Sun was not created yet, so the "day" referred to in the mystical language of Genesis was a "division" of creation, not the literal day we refer to on the calendar.

The concept of God in the Kabbalah is that God is a verb; and more precisely a transitive verb, the verb of Being. So it is reasonable to believe that all which emanates from God is also a transitive verb of Being. The energy of Being radiates out to create the power of thought, the power of emotion and is then expressed in the actions of the world of doing. This is the link that explains that action completes faith in the Kabbalistic Life. Faith does not affect this world for good until it is linked to an action, for truly it is not in this world until it is an action. This concept of action in time and space completing faith is expressed in the construction and use of the Hebrew language itself.

Biblical Hebrew is based upon the action; the verb is the base form of a word. For instance, the verb "to write" is *katav*, with the K – T – V as the roots of the word. Words that have to do with writing are formed upon that basic root: to correspond – *hitkatev*; a written marriage document is a *ketubbah*; and a written letter is a *miktav*. The verb is the basic form in Biblical Hebrew. Because of the emphasis of the verb, in Biblical Hebrew syntax the verb is generally place first in the sentence. This is to the effect that the first piece of information you receive in a sentence is WHAT was done, then WHO did it, and how. Hebrew tradition is based on action – because that is how anything becomes present in this World of Assiyah. Before anything is expressed in action it doesn't exist here in this world!

The concept of action as the primary characteristic of this world is even inherent in the concept of perfection and imperfection in Biblical Hebrew. Perfect and Imperfect are tenses in Biblical Hebrew. There are only two options called "Perfect" and "Imperfect" for time orientation. Perfect tense is when the action is finished. "Yesterday I went to the store" is perfect tense. Imperfect tense simply means the action is currently happening or will happen in the future. "I am going to the store now" and "Tomorrow I will go to the store" both use imperfect tense of the verb. The theology is brilliant! It relieves us of the struggle for perfection defined as "without blemish or error" and allows us to attain the state of perfection for simply having finished something! Good, bad, or ugly, if something is finished it is "perfect". This gives new meaning to the bumper sticker "Be patient. God isn't finished with me yet!"

The concept of Perfect and Imperfect tense is used to imply God as outside of time and space interacting with us in our lives within time and space. When a Prophet of the Biblical period is giving God's words of prophecy to the people, the text is pointed in Perfect tense, even though it is foretelling something that hasn't happened yet, which is Imperfect tense! The reasoning is that if God said this is going to happen, it is as if it has already happened, because God is in the "Eternal

Now" speaking to us here in time and space through the Prophet's words. The use of the grammar of the language implies the Prophet's faith in God. Assiyah, the World of Action, is the first world of finite dimensions of time and space. In Assiyah, we bring together the Infinite and the Finite, through the transformers of our mind, heart and actions.

Have you ever experienced having a great idea, and then suddenly there were some conflicting feelings, emotions about it? You love the idea, but you are also fearful. What actions do you take when you are caught between your love and excitement and your fear? There usually are none. You don't move one way or another. You go back and forth between your head and your heart, your excitement and your fear, your thoughts of empowerment and your thoughts of catastrophic disaster. Your love connects you to thought which give rise to steps of action that will manifest the idea. Your fearful emotions hold you in your place, your actions frozen. This is what the phrase "frozen by fear" means. When you stand in your fear, or go back and forth between your fear and your love you can not move forward in your actions. Once you make a choice to stand in your love in the face of your fear– then your actions will bring your idea into reality in the world. But exactly how are the Infinite Worlds of Atzilut, B'riyah and Yetzirah transformed into the physical World of Assiyah through actions?

Spiritual Assiyah and Physical Assiyah

The World of Assiyah is different from Yetzirah, B'riyah and Atzilut in that it is subdivided into two parts. There is Spiritual Assiyah and there is Physical Assiyah. You can understand this easily when you think of your own self as a human being. You are not only the physi-

cal body, but there are other parts of you that interact with Life, name-
ly the thoughts of your mind and the feelings of your heart. While we
have spoken of thoughts and feelings in relationship to Infinity as the
Worlds of B'riyah and Yetzirah, we must differentiate our mind and
our heart from the Infinite Worlds of B'riyah and Yetzirah, for our
mind and heart is part of the finite World of Assiyah, action. The
Worlds we spoke of previously are Higher Dimensions, are Infinite
and radiate their Light through filters **onto and into** the World of
Assiyah. Yet we find we have thoughts and feelings within ourselves
as human beings, created beings of this Dimension of Assiyah. This is
why we separate our **human** mind thoughts and human heart feelings
and call them SA, Spiritual Assiyah, intangible thoughts and feelings
that become actions in the World of Action. The elemental body which
we use to express those actions is called Physical Assiyah, or PA. I
will be using SA and PA for thoughts and feelings in the finite World
of Assiyah.

Spiritual Assiyah is the spiritual part of you which is non-tangible.
Can you touch a thought? Can you touch a feeling? No. But you can
touch others with a thought or with your feelings – **if you express it
through your body in an action!** While it is a thought in your head,
or a feeling in your heart it exists in Spiritual Assiyah, SA. There is a
huge difference between the Infinite B'riyah and Yetsirah and your
SA. The Infinite Dimensions are a higher vibration of energy closer in
formation to the Source than the SA of finite Assiyah. Your thoughts
are very subject to the chemical and hormonal balance within your
brain (physical PA), and your emotions are affected directly by those
same factors. How much rest you have had, what is going on in the
energy around you, and your age and maturity all affect your thoughts
and feelings. The Infinite Worlds of B'riyah and Yetzirah are not

affected by these factors. This integrated finite being of SA and PA is what I refer to as your Incarnate Self. This is who you are in this incarnation, this embodiment of your SA (Spiritual Assiyah) and your body (Physical Assiyah).

To be able to use the concept of Spiritual Assiyah with more detail, I break SA down even further into the two areas: thoughts, SA-B'riyah and feelings, SA-Yetzirah. The SA prefix signifies the finite thoughts and feelings as you experience them in this incarnation. Your SA is a consciousness that you have in awareness of the world around you. When you shift your consciousness to the Infinite Yetzirah and B'riyah, you tap into resources beyond your own Incarnate Self and access the resources of your Authentic Soul (Eternal Being). As you can see, your SA is so integrated with your PA as to be inter-dependent. However integrated and interdependent your Incarnate Self consciousness is, you are not limited to it, for with practice you can shift your consciousness to transcend to the Higher Dimensions.

Another way of understanding SA is to understand SA B'riyah as intelligence and SA Yetzirah as attachments. Remember, we are not limiting the World of Assiyah to the human experience. Assiyah is all that exists in the physical world. Therefore, all that exists here has an intelligence and attachments that belong to the spiritual as well as form or embodiment that is physical. Birds have an intelligence that enables them to build a nest and migrate. There are birds and animals who mate for Life, and who remain within their flock or "society" for Life. Elephants organize themselves in a way that protects all of the young. Even the oceans, mountains and land masses have an intelligence which alters their growth and formations according to conditions. My sister was married to a man who climbed mountains and specialized in ice climbing. He summated Mt. Everest. He says that climbing a mountain is about forming an intimate relationship with the mountain... each mountain either lets you climb her or not. In the extreme activity of moving across the face of the seemingly impossible to cross, the Divine in the human spirit opens to the Divine in the mountain. The perception goes far beyond the physical presence and enters the spiritual presence. This is the World of Spiritual Assiyah.

Your body, PA, is your elemental expression in the physical world. It is not your Authentic Soul, your Eternal Being, but it is an emanation and expression of it. Is your reflection in a mirror you? Your Authentic Soul projects out an Incarnate Self, it is not all of you, but a reflection as it were of the part of your Authentic Soul that is called for to fulfill your destiny in this finite Lifetime. Your PA is part of that projection/reflection.

Your PA is elemental because your body is made up of the elements of Mother Earth. If you break down the chemical compounds within your flesh and blood body you will find the elements and body of Mother Earth.

Your body also has a consciousness of its own as well. Part of body consciousness (or body intelligence) for instance is your body's ability to digest food. You do not give conscious thought to digesting your food. It is a function of the consciousness of your body. You do not think of each heart beat or tell your glands how much or when to send out certain hormones to keep your body in a state of balance. Your SA mind does not tell your body when to start or stop the rhythms of menses, menarche or menopause, but your body's intelligence in your brain does! Your body's intelligence or consciousness regulate those functions to stay alive, maintain in wholeness and even to contribute to the proLiferation of humanity. The meditations at the end of the last chapter will help you open your consciousness to the intelligence of your body! This is part of the work of imagery and visualization for healing in your body. You will even learn how to interact with your body and love and nurture your body.

How can Infinite B'riyah or Infinite Yetzirah come into the physical, finite world? It comes through the empowerment of your Spiritual Assiyah and the expressions of your Physical Assiyah. This is true of all of Creation. Birds, fishes, land animals, oceans, streams, forests, deserts. There is an element of SA the Spirit of the Creation and the PA the physical element of the Creation. Remember the meditation on the tree? In meditation you can open up to feel the Spirit Life of the tree, the Life-force coursing through it. That is the SA. The bark, leaves and limbs is the PA.

I was driving in South Florida one summer day when the winds were picking up in front of an afternoon summer thunderstorm. There were wide open fields on either side of the road which were bordered by long rows of Cedars of Lebanon, tall cone shaped evergreens. As the wind crossed the road the trees began to bend and sway. However, instead of all the trees bowing at once with the wind, I noticed that side by side, the trees were bending in turn, every other tree together! These were bending, and then these were bending; these were bending and then these were bending. It looked like they were praying or davvening together, bending in motion and rhythm to their prayers. It is easy to imagine that the pathways of the wind had a play, yet, when my SA opened to the rhythm of the SA of the trees, it was as if we were dancing or praying together. And the wind was our fiddler – or prayer leader! I could not have seen or experienced the wind without the PA of the trees, and my own PA in coordination together.

Go back to Chapter One and the Circle of Being exercise you did. Your Circle of Being is in the Higher Dimensions, and the rays of expressions (your actions, the things you do) of your Being are emanated through your SA and PA. Your elemental body is an **expression** or ray of that Circle of Being, while your Authentic Soul **is** the Circle of Being. In the image of God, the Emanator, you too, have emanated who you are in this Lifetime.

We have learned about the Four Worlds, Atzilut – Emanation, B'riyah – Intellect, Yetzirah – Emotion, and Assiyah – Actions, which has two parts, SA, Spiritual Assiyah and PA, Physical Assiyah. This is a valuable framework onto which you will be able to hang a sophisticated matrix of information and understanding in the future. It is expandable and it bears further study. To understand more about these Four Worlds, we can differentiate the factors of the Infinite and the Finite.

Three Factors

The World of Assiyah (World of Action) can be divided into three factors. Each of the Worlds carries these three factors, but in understanding the difference between the worlds you will see the difference between these factors. In Assiyah, there are the three factors called "space" ("world" in the old tradition), "time" ("year" in the old tradition) and "self" ("soul" in the old tradition). These three factors define the Dimension of Action. **Time** is a factor in our actions, **space** is a factor in our actions and our **self** is a factor in our actions. Self can mean me, it can mean you, it can mean that mountain over there, or the desert, the Sun, Moon or Universe. All three of these factors in some way integrate and play on action in the World of Assiyah. Everything in action is involved with time; everything in action is involved with space, everything in action is involved with a self of some sort.

To take action we must utilize a space. If you don't have any space you can't move.

That action takes time. Time is the overlay of measurement of how long an action takes to complete. Every 24 hours each part of our planet has a time of darkness and a time of light from the Sun. Each action takes a unit of time.

The one acting is self. There has to be an "act-or" to perform the action.

There are some illusions that we (self) can experience in relation to time and space. Have you noticed that it seems the older you get the faster time "goes by"? Is time really traveling? Abraham Joshua Heschel gives us the following wonderful example of the illusory nature of time in his book *The Sabbath*. In paraphrase, there was a man traveling by train. At first the train pulled out of the station very slowly. With each turn of the wheels the train traveled faster and faster. Soon the man noticed that the telephone poles along the side of the tracks were flying by! Were the telephone poles really "flying by"? They were rooted in the ground by a measure of feet. He was flying by! It was the man who was moving forward faster, not the poles. It took less time to pass each pole. So it is with time. The busier our day, the more we are doing, or the more we shift our consciousness in concentration, the "faster" time seems to go. We use microwaves, high speed internet, faster cars, planes and trains, the younger generation even talks really fast! We move from activity to activity faster, so we feel like we are pushed for lack of time. It is we who are doing the pushing! It is we who have shifted, not time. We rarely take time to "do nothing". The activities of the world are quickening. We are revving up the actions which are taking less time. How do you feel when you sit at a red light, wait in line at the store or are watching the clock on the microwave heat your coffee to scalding – in one minute!

We are impatient. We want to move forward, get going, get to the next activity. The world still takes a certain time to rotate and revolve around the Sun. But we are putting many more actions in that same length of time – and it feels like there is less time, and that time is moving faster. It is a measure of our actions!

Essential Factors of the World of Physical Assiyah – Action

Space

Time

Self

In the Infinite Worlds of B'riyah and Yetzirah these three factors differ to describe the essence of that Dimension. **Space** parallels **Mansions, (Group or Field)**. **Time** is paralleled by **Change**. And **Self** is paralleled by **Soul**.

Since there is no physical form in the Higher Dimensions, the factor of mansions takes the place of space. Modern Kabbalists also name this factor groups or fields. To understand the term group or field, consider what a group or field is in the physical and natural world. We categorize birds in specific groups, such as water birds, birds of prey and migrating birds. We say a person of high abilities in his or her profession is "outstanding in their field." We do not have to define the field, because it is not time or space, but it denotes characteristics. What identifies these groups or fields is an abstract idea of qualities. This is an example of how "mansion" or "group" is used. This is the sense in which we use the terms group, field or mansion in the World of Yetzirah and the World of B'riyah.

In centuries past those who studied the Kabbalah were called the "reapers of the field". Now you can understand the mystical meaning of that name. The entire Book of Ruth is set around the "reapers of the field". In the Book of Matthew Jesus is reported to have explained a parable's symbols, naming the world as the Field and the Angels as the reapers. He was applying to this world the mystical terminology of the Higher Worlds. You may recall that in John 14:2, Jesus said, "In my Father's house are many mansions..." In the mystic traditions he was referring to the groups or fields in the Higher Worlds outside of this world of time and space.

Just as there is not space, but there is field, in the Infinite Worlds, so time is paralleled by change in the Infinite.

There is a transformation from the factor of time in the World of Assiyah to the factor of the process of change in the Higher Dimensions. Remembering that the Higher Dimensions are energy in form, it is the energy that undergoes change. This is referring to the pure essence of change or the potential for change.

In the physical world time is the measuring unit for action – which denotes change. If something is in motion it is in change. In the Higher Worlds, the factor is directly the change itself. In the World of B'riyah, for instance, a powerful thought can change and time is not a factor.

Have you ever been in prayer or meditation and suddenly you realize you have an entire concept from beginning to end without the process of one thought moving to the next in your head? You get the whole thing at once. Yet, nothing in this world has changed except YOU! Afterwards it might take two hours to write out in linear language what you received in a nanosecond of non-thinking consciousness. When you have that experience you have reached into the World of B'riyah, the power of Intellect and there is no time involvement, only change – for you have changed by gaining this information and will never again be the same. What has changed in you is your perspective. It has come to you and through you from outside of you, from the Higher Dimensions.

By way of metaphor, once you have tasted chocolate how can you go back to the state of not knowing the taste of chocolate? You are forever changed by the experience. This illustrates the nature of the factor of change rather than time in the Higher Dimensions.

Relative and essential to change and field is the elemental factor of Soul.

Much the same way that Self is the self-consciousness of the physical world, "Soul" is the term for the Infinite self-consciousness within the factors of "mansion" and "change." The Self of this physical world becomes Soul in the Higher Worlds. In this incarnation, your Self is finite. However, your Soul in the Higher Dimensions is Eternal. At some point your Incarnate Self consciousness will disengage from the physical body and will transcend back up into the Higher Dimensions to your Authentic Soul, your Eternal Being. This is the consciousness of Soul. It has emanated your Incarnate Self and will receive it at the fulfillment of your days in the World of Assiyah.

Have you ever had the experience of meeting someone for the first time and feeling that you already know them? This is called "Soul Recognition" for your Soul from the Higher Dimensions recognizes their Soul from the Higher Dimensions. You may be meeting their Self in this incarnation Lifetime for the first time, and their personality and characteristics may be foreign, but their eyes tell you "we have met." Many times this happens when we are completing karmic relationships with others in this Lifetime. Sometimes you can recognize someone with whom you had a very close relationship to in another time and place (outside of this Lifetime) and you desire to bond again, however, it would be inappropriate to the relationship you have in this time and space and Lifetime. It is so valuable to recognize this experience so you can connect with their Soul and keep the relationship in a way that upholds your highest intentions for your Self and the other person in this Lifetime.

Sometimes the Soul Mate feeling is exactly that – your Souls have been together in Eternity and will continue the relationship in the physical World of Assiyah. These are relationships that last a Lifetime. Sometimes these partners or friends are so close they begin to reflect each other, or look alike, manifesting their blending of Light physically. These relationships are marked by ease, contentment and passion. Passion alone is not an indication, but the relationship carries an easy comfort level and a sense of contentment in the presence of the other person as well. These are the most blessed relationships to enjoy in our lives.

The Archangel MichaEl is an essence of consciousness that is distinct from but integral to the framework and backdrop of the World of B'riyah. There are other created Beings in the Infinite Worlds which we will explore in the next section. Just as Self is an essence of consciousness in the Finite World, Soul is an essence of consciousness in the Infinite Worlds.

Essential Factors of the Worlds of B'riyah and Yetzirah

Change

Mansion, Field, or Group

Soul

I want to make a distinction at this point between the terms Infinite and Eternal. *Webster's New Dictionary* defines Infinite as: 1. having ιit or extending indefinitely. 2. vast. Eternal is defined as: lasting forever. These two words are often used interchangeably in conversation; however, for purposes of understanding the factors of the physical and non-physical dimensions, I would like to use Infinite to refer to an alternative to space and Eternal as an alternative to time. Therefore, in the Higher Dimensions of B'riyah and Yetzirah my Soul is Infinite (endless resource) and is Eternal (timeless). While my Self in this world is finite in physical form and is on a timetable of maturity. Bringing these two together, Soul in the Infinite and Self in the Finite enables me to be the conduit for bringing Energy into physicality, Infinite into Finite and Eternal into Time. God's love made manifest in physical form ~ you and I.

In its essence the World of Atzilut, emanation is not a world at all, for it is the All One. There is no factor within Atzilut, for there is nothing to stand in its field or group, there is nothing to transform or change. We cannot even say "all One" for all would declare a necessary "each" and there is no each. It is One, All the Light of Being. It is The Source and The Destiny.

How do we use these factors in everyday Life?

The Higher Dimensions of B'riyah and Yetzirah have a factor of change, but those changes take place outside of time. They are in the Eternal Now, that is, what we think of as future in this world is Now, in the Higher Dimensions; and what we think of as past is also Now. The events of the physical world of past present and future exist in the Higher Dimensions as the Always Now, or Eternal Now.

Understanding this enables you to draw on the Higher Dimensions when you are making choices for your Life. For instance, when you fear something in your Life you rob yourselves of the energy of the moment of Now in this Dimension, because fear is ALWAYS of the future. Make a list of three things you fear. Look at each item on the list and ask yourself, "Is this going on right now? Is this something of the future?" Every item on your list is most likely something you fear will happen in the future. You are only given energy to live the moment of Now in this Dimension. When you hold fears and thoughts connected to the emotion of fear there is no energy for it because it is in the future, and the future is not yet here in this Dimension, so there is no energy for it. The only energy you have is the energy you have in this moment of Now. It is akin to breathing. You cannot breathe for next week; you can only breathe for the moment of now, now, and now. Your energy for living, the flow of your Life-force is the same way. That is the only available energy with which you are holding your fears. That robs you of the energy to live fully in the "moment of now." Sometimes your fears can be so pervasive that you miss the current moment altogether. Holding your fear with the energy of the moment can leave you feeling drained, for it has leaked out trying to hold the future in the now. But you have a choice.

Fear is a natural part of the human experience; so how can you use your fear for good in your Life? You can use your fear as a flag reminding you that you have a choice: you can stand in your love or stand in your fear. But, ultimately it is your choice. Fear and love are the same continuum; love is at a high vibrational energy and fear is at the other end at a very low level of vibrational energy. That is why we use the phrase, "Frozen in your fear." Fear stops action. Your choice is what empowers you. Every moment you make a choice of what to use your energy for, thoughts connecting to love or fear. Your fear has thoughts attached to them as does your love. Which thoug
choose to hold? If you hold to your thoughts of love, the

return to the moment of now and your fears dissipate. Your energy flows to you moment by moment; you can choose how to use it.

Understanding the concepts of the three factors of the Infinite Dimensions and the factors of the Finite enables you to use the spiritual tool of moving your consciousness out beyond time and space to make your choices based in the Eternal Now of the Higher Dimensions where your Authentic Soul (Eternal Being) exists. As you focus on your Authentic Soul, in the Eternal Now, you can use the wisdom you access from that perspective to lay to rest your fears – because wisdom dissipates the fear and employs your patience. Your Authentic Soul knows that the events of your Life are in Divine Order, while your Incarnate Self's mind may be experiencing chaos. Declaring this state of Divine Order offers a paradigm shift for your way of thinking.

In your SA (Spiritual Assiyah – mind and heart) the three factors of the Higher Dimensions are infused with the factors of the World of Action. For instance, does a thought take any space? No. A thought is an energy that moves in the "space" of your mind. In that way your mind is the transformer to bring the energy from the Infinite into the Finite. Does your love require space? No, however, you bring it into the physical world of Assiyah, through your actions. For instance, it takes no space for you to **feel** love for your child and **think** about hugging them. However, to put an action to this feeling and thought requires space, for you must draw near to them physically and then extend your arms around them to embrace them! The Infinite love flowing through you has manifested in your actions in the world.

Infinite and Finite Worlds

Infinite Worlds

Atzilut – Emanation, Undifferentiated Being raying out

B'riyah – Power of Intellect

Yetzirah – Power of Emotion

Finite World

Assiyah – Actions, Physical World

> **Spiritual Assiyah** – Intelligence (Instinct) and Feelings (Attachment)
>
> **Physical Assiyah** – Body, physicality

Comparison of Essential Factors of the Infinite and Finite Worlds

Assiyah	B'riyah & Yetzirah
Time	Change
Space	Mansion, Field, Group
Self	Soul

Created Beings of the Higher Realms

The mystical teachings of Abraham include Beings who are resident in the Higher Dimensions. These created Beings from Yetzirah and B'riyah are called the *Malachim* in the Hebrew, which literally means "messengers." In English we call them the Angels. The word *Malach* (singular for Malachim) simply means messenger, for these Beings are the messengers carrying the Divine Plenty between the Worlds. The Divine Plenty includes the messages of Divine Guidance and Wisdom delivered to individuals in the World of Assiyah.

So what do you suppose the created beings of the World of B'riyah, pure intellect would be? They are the brightest of beings, carrying Light that is one step away from Atzilut, the totality of All. This is the realm of the Archangels. They are beings of pure intellect, the power of thought. They too are subject to the factors of their Dimension, "mansions" and "change". They are of the world of pure mind. Their energy is brighter, more translucent, higher in vibrations and purer having less distortion from The Source.

The World of B'riyah is also referred to as the "world of the Throne" or "Throne room" and the Chariot. It is the closest to the place of emanation. The Archangels as messengers from this proximity to The Source are our contact with the ultimate Source. This Dimension is the crossroads of the dialogue between The One and The Many. It is the first differentiation. The Archangels transfer and transform the Divine Plenty from The Source to the Worlds below. The highest secrets or Divine Mysteries reside in this realm. It is the destiny of those desiring to be open in consciousness to the fullest in this incarnation, for anything higher would result in undifferentiation and could not sustain the differentiated human experience. In this crossroads "throne room" all knowledge of that which is and that which will be is open in the Light. It is here the "reaper of the fields" comes to the experience of Awe, a glimpse ever so swift of all Being One and yet being a part of the All One. It is not easily accessible, let alone sustain within the human consciousness. The Archangels thereby effect a Presence of that Dimension in dialogue with the human consciousness which sustains the open channels. The created beings of this

Dimension are called in the Hebrew *Seraphim* which is the plural of *Seraph*. This word literally translates "fiery one". They "burn" with the Divine Light. They are able to lift the "reaper of the field" to a consciousness of The One to higher and higher degrees. The lower one descends into the Worlds the more of an illusion of separation there becomes. From the "throne room" there is a very thin veil between Beings. Yet the filter or screen between the World of B'riyah and Atzilut is the greatest of all. To leap beyond B'riyah into Atzilut is to dissipate all differentiality, all uniqueness, and all emanation of Soul.

The World of B'riyah, the World of Thought, is home to the Archangels such as MichaEl, RaphaEl, GavriEl, UriEl and RaziEl and the Seraphim, the Fiery Angels who surround the Throne – or the portal of Emanation. The "Throne room" is symbolic language for the highest mansion of Emanation. The Archangels and Seraphim are created of an extremely high vibration of Light. They have given us names to call them by in order for us to focus our energy when we summon them. Each Archangel's name ends in EL which is a name for God. This direct attachment signifies their high ranking in the hierarchy of the Divine Beings. They do not need names for each other, for they are in an open state of consciousness. They not only recognize each other's energy, but communicate without the constraints of time or place.

Names of the Archangels and their Meanings
Archangel MichaEL – Angel of Awe

His name literally means "Who is like unto God?" When we ponder this question, "Who is like God?" we open to the Awe of God's indescribable Presence. Archangel MichaEL brings that Presence near with it the luminous experience.

MichaEL is often depicted with a sword in his hand. For this reason it is often mistakenly thought that he is an Angel of war. In actuality, Archangel MichaEL is present when humanity comes into conflict and there is much blood shed to bring a balancing energy. The oft recorded miracles that happen in times of war and the "foxhole conversions" or spiritual experience that those in war retell is evidence of the presence of Archangel MichaEL. When you have that "moment of Awe" or "mountaintop experience" it is Archangel MichaEL who is opening the energy of the nearness and presence of The One to you. "Who is like unto God?" and then you experience the power of the The One, and the grace all at once. Archangel MichaEL is also the Angel of Compassion, for when we experience and extend compassion, conflict is resolved. Archangel MichaEL is often a leading Angel in a company of Angelic hosts and one of the most powerful in God's "cabinet" of Angels. MichaEL is open to your questions and delights in delivering the messages that answer your prayers and questions, for in doing so he is serving The Light to which he is devoted. Archangel MichaEL is with us to see the Spiritual Growth of this Dimension in Light, Peace, and Love.

Archangel UriEL – Angel of the Light of God

The Archangel UriEL's name means "My Light is God. The Hebrew word Or, is the root of this name which means "light". He is the Angel of Illumination. His Effulgent Light is a direct channel for the Divine Light which we need in concentration, measure and intensity that we need at that moment of our Life. Whenever you need Light to find your pathway in Life you can call on UriEL whose Light is Truth.

Archangel RaphaEL – Angel of Healing

A *rophe* in Hebrew is a doctor. RaphaEL is the Angel of Healing. When you are in need of healing, either in body, emotions, mental or spiritual, RaphaEL is the Archangel who brings the messages of healing energy, the Divine Plenty of healing to you. He is also the Angel of Love, for in love do we heal. It is through love that we heal our world.

Archangel RaziEL

Razi in Hebrew is a secret, therefore, RaziEL is the Angel of the Divine Mysteries. When you enter the "secret hiding place of the Most High" (Ps. 91:1) you are in the realm of RaziEL. As Ps. 91:11 continues:

The Holy One will give the Angels charge to keep you in all your ways.
Psalm 91:11

As you seek the mysteries of the Holy One and receive understanding it is Archangel RaziEL who brings the Divine Plenty of these mysteries to you. Have you ever had a moment when you suddenly understood a concept or truth that was hidden to you previously? This is the work of RaziEL. He is the Keeper of the Divine Secrets.

Archangel GavriEL

In Hebrew the word *gibor* means strength, so Archangel GabriEL is the Angel of God's Strength. GavriEL brings the Divine Plenty of Strength through the Dimensions to your Life. The next time you need strength call upon GavriEL to keep you on your path.

Chapter Two, "Spiritual Practices for Miraculous Living" in the book, *You Called My Name, The Hidden Treasures of Your Hebrew Heritage* will give you further information on the Angels. You can learn how to open up to the Archangels and set them around you with a visual and guided meditation on my CD "Opening to the Light of the Archangels".

The Divine Beings created within the World of Yetzirah are Angels, Ministering Spirits, Guardian Angels, Elementals, Ophanim (Winged Beings), Cheruvim (who draw close to us to draw us close to God), and conscious beings each carrying a particular impulse. They live within their consciousness to fulfill their incentive, their tendency or inclination and the inspirations sent as messages. They interact with the Worlds above and below them to move the Divine Plenty. This was symbolized by the dream of Jacob when he saw a ladder with Angels ascending and descending on it in Genesis 28:12.

Remember the factor in the Higher Dimension of "fields? When there are groups or fields of Angels moving together, they are called a "camp of Angels." For instance, there may be a camp of Angels of love. There are infinite types of love – no two alike. There are infinite degrees of these types of love, however, there is a totality of the emotion that brings these created beings, Angels together to move in a purpose for change, transference. These Angels act, create, interact, communicate and flow with their essence of emotion within their World of Yetzirah, emotion. This Dimension is the power plant if you remember for the World of B'riyah, the World of Intellect, or thought.

The nature of an Angel is to be a contact between the World of Assiyah, Action and the Higher Worlds. This is their essence and fulfillment of being. They serve to carry the Higher Light to the Lower Worlds, and to take the energy from the Lower Worlds into the Higher

Dimensions. Angels carry out missions as they are sent from the Higher Dimensions to the World of Assiyah. They are sometimes robed in the garments of the human form and sometimes they are felt as a Presence. They can be heard as well as sometimes seen. Often when they are appearing in human form the person seeing them or interacting with them is not aware that they are talking with an Angel. They are sometimes perceived as an energy form, without defined physical form. They can also change or transform themselves to some other form before the perceiver's eyes.

This was the case in the story of Manoah, the father of Samson, from the Bible. He knew there was something special about this man he was interacting with. But, when the man turned into a pillar of fire he got it! The guy is an Angel, a Divine Being from another dimension who is not subject to the factors and physical laws of the World of Assiyah. Remember that transformation (change) is a factor of the Angelic Realm, rather than time. Even when they are appearing in this physical world of time and space they are not bound by time and space, for they are Created Beings of the Higher Dimensions beyond those factors. That is why they are so helpful to us in our human experience to help us make the transformations of our lives. Yes, there are Angels that do not carry the Higher Light. They are of lesser light and they have specific purposes and intentions in their existence in the larger picture of Creation, as well.

The created Beings in the World of Yetzirah, the World of Emotion, are Messengers carrying the pure essence of emotion. Each created Being is a particular emotion, carried at a particular degree and quality. They are conscious of themselves and of each other. They are conscious of the Worlds around them and their purposes in those Worlds.

"An Angel, however, is not merely a fragment of existence doing nothing more than manifesting an emotion; it is a whole and integral being, conscious of itself and its surroundings and able to act and create and do things within the framework of the world of formation (feelings). The nature of the Angel is to be, to a degree, as its name in Hebrew signifies, a messenger, to constitute a permanent contact between our world of action and the higher worlds. The Angel is the one who effects transfers of the vital plenty between worlds."
Thirteen Petalled Rose, Pg. 9

Angels carry only one message at a time. We are taught this by the events of the story of Abraham who was visited by three angels in Genesis 18:1. One of the three angels delivers the message to Abraham that he and Sarah, his wife, are to have a child at that time next year. The other two angels are carrying messages to be delivered to the cities of Sodom and Amorah (Gomorrah). The story continues in Genesis 19:1. The scene changes to Sodom and there are now only two Angels, for only two messages are yet to be delivered. Each Angel holds the energy of a particular message.

Angels come to help our Souls when we are in transition at death. The Angel is said to have the name of the person they are to help. Sometimes, when a person is critically ill it is a tradition to change their name – so the Angel cannot take them because that is not the name the Angel's message holds. Many times the name *Khayyim* (male) or *Khayah* (female) is added because this name means "Life". For example, if an Angel came to find the Soul of Avraham ben Terah and his loved ones, fearing for his Life due to an illness changed his name to Avraham Khayyim ben Terah, then the message that it is time for the Soul to transcend, leaving the body and the World of Action behind, could not be delivered, and the person should live. One Angel, one message. Now, that is not to say that there may not be an Angel that comes with that new name in another hour, and the person may still transcend. But, the message going out to the Universe by the name change is that not everyone connected to this Soul is ready for them to leave. There may be varying amounts of time given to that person, but when it is time, and that person's treasured number of days are spent, their Soul will transition into the Higher Dimensions, back into their Authentic Soul, and the Angels will accompany them (often with loved ones from the other side of the Veil) in Divine Order. It happens that sometimes our loved ones leave our lives before we are ready. The readiness is in our Incarnate Minds and Hearts, our SA, but on a Soul level, we know, we may grieve, but we know. If we think back on things they said over the last 40 days of their lives we will often hear the "goodbyes of their Soul"; things that they said to us that were appropriate at the time, but were said a little differently and carried meaning in retrospect to their transition. We treasure those Soul messages they gave us; it doesn't hurt any less, but it is comforting to know it was in Divine Order, there was a purpose beyond our own Self.

Angels bring messages, but they also live in consciousness of themselves, each other, the Higher Dimensions and this Dimension.

Some Angels are created from the beginning such as the Archangels, and Seraphim. It is as if they are hardwired in. Other angels are created dynamically through the actions of human beings. One of the dynamic ways an Angel is created is when a human being does a mitzvah, a good deed, be it an action or a prayer for someone, or even a loving thought sent mentally to someone, an Angel is created from that energy which moves the emotion of that deed, feeling or thought to the intended recipient. The Angel remains "attached" by energy to the sender, because the Angel is made from the energy imprint (which is like a spiritual finger print) of the vibrational patterns unique to the sender. That is why there is truth to the saying "What goes around comes around." Actually, you might say "What goes around never left the sender." So we create Angels from the emotions we send out to others. If we have negative feelings such as hatred, jealousy or anger toward another person that creates an Angel of a lower vibrational energy that attaches us to that person and continually connects us with them in negative energy. We are attached to others by the Angels we create throughout our lives. The question is what emotional Angels do we choose to create around us and between ourselves and others?

Negative emotions that you hold for another person are attached to you, and lower your own energy. If you have created an Angel between yourself and someone else, which is carrying the energy of a negative emotion, you can change this by raising the level of the Angel by your intentions. So how do you rid your Life of the lower vibrational Angels that you may have created? You can raise the level of Light in that Angel through surrender, release and forgiveness.

If someone has truly hurt you it may be far from your intentions to forgive them even if you want to for the sake of peace. Would it make a difference to you if you could just forgive the person's Soul, and not worry about the action; what they did that hurt you? Your forgiveness is directed toward the person. The actions of what they have done are God's to deal with, because only God can see the heart (it is God's emanation) and only the Holy One of Mercy and Justice can know the harmony to be restored in the whole picture. It is our ability to respond with grace, compassion and mercy. That is then the attributes we draw upon from the Holy One for our own injustices toward others.

When I studied Latin in school I remember the scenes of the gladiatorial contests described. When a gladiator pinned his opponent at the point of death he would raise his eyes to the spectators to take direction from their wishes – was his opponent to live signaled by a thumbs up or die, signified by the thumbs down? You can think of forgiveness as the same choice. You are standing before God, the Creator of all Life – are you for-giving this Soul Life? By extending forgiveness you are not condoning what they have done, you are simply standing before God saying, "Give him / her Life!" By so doing, you have raised the vibrations of the Angel between you and that person. You are ready to take a deep breath and continue the process of integrating your feelings with that person further if so needed.

You can process what you are angry about (or whatever the negative emotion is). There are a number of ways of doing this. You can do the meditation "Thou Preparest a Table before Me" which is a meditation for healing relationships. If you would like a CD of this meditation please contact me.

Thou Preparest a Table Before Me

Meditation given by

Rabbi Zalman Schachter-Shalomi

In this meditation, take a deep breath and relax. Then envision the Presence of God, however you sense the Divine, and envision a table of all your favorite things, prepared in your honor. Seated around the table, picture everyone from your Life who has hurt you in some way, including the person you want to process your feelings about.

Ask that person to stand up. Speak with the Soul (not the Incarnate Self) of that other person. Tell him or her how you feel, why you feel that way, and ask them any questions you have for them.

When you have finished be quiet for a few moments and listen to their soul's reply to you, remembering that you are in the Presence of the Holy One. You may find out more about a situation than you understood in the natural world.

After they have finished listen to the Voice of the Holy One speaking to you for wisdom and guidance in this matter.

Speak to the Holy One in the Light you are then standing in at that moment.

If you have been asked to do something decide what your answer is to God.
Spend as much time in that place as you desire.

When you feel complete, come back into the consciousness of the room in which you are sitting and think about your experiences.

Take a first step in doing what you decided you desire to do.

At this point, can you say that you are for-giving that person Life, allowing the actions of the person to be God's business?

Another way to process some of your feelings about a person is to simply lift him or her up in your vision, and put him or her into a great urn that the Angels hold for you to release and surrender all you desire to give over to them. We are talking about human emotions which are the power plant of your Life! Sometimes it is just not that easy to let go of them. If you are having difficulty letting go you can ask Archangel MichaEL to help you. Where do you feel this in your body? Picture scooping all that nasty energy out of your body and ask MichaEL to help you get rid of those feelings. And Archangel MichaEL will honor your request.

Close your eyes and envision an Angel holding a huge urn.

Then envision the person you have a problem with.

Take them into your cupped hands, lift them up and release them into the Angel's urn.

Surrender all your feelings for them into the urn at the same time.

Watch with your visionary (3rd) eye to see what happens when all of that energy goes into the urn. Whatever you see happen to him or her and your feelings directly relates to what is going on in the energy realms with the two of you.

You are now released of your feelings and are free to choose to bless that person with Life.

You do not have to forgive **what** they did, just stand in witness to God that you are "for-giving them Life" – that is forgiveness. You can say something like, "God bless you and send you Light that you may fulfill your Destiny in Peace." Remember, you are not condoning what they did. Leave that in the hands of God for equity. You are sending them Light for a higher pathway. Then, the Angel you have created is one of Light and Blessings – which attaches Light and Blessing to you, as well!

Have you ever been in traffic and had someone cut in front of you or nearly cause you to have an accident? When you get angry with them and utter words of anger you are creating an Angel! This is a great opportunity to change your words of fear and anger to a blessing! Dr. Neil Rand suggests that whenever that happens to you in traffic take the opportunity to bless them with words such as "Please bless that person with Light and may they get where they are going in safety." Blessings create very high vibrational Angels who then carry that blessing of the Divine Plenty across the Dimensions.

By the same token, whenever someone is kind or courteous to me in traffic I like to send them a blessing asking God to bless them for they have blessed me with kindness. Again, you have taken the opportunity to create a beautiful Angel of Blessing, adding to the Light between you and others.

The Archangels, Seraphim, Ophanim, Guardian Angels, Elementals (those who care for the elements of the planet) and ministering spirits are conscious Beings of the Higher Dimensions who are messengers of the Divine Plenty and bring Light, joy, wisdom and fun into our lives. They are powerful and precious. They honor us and acknowledge the difficulty of the human experience. They are there whenever we focus our consciousness on them and by the Grace of the Holy One, they are there even when we are not aware of them. Open your heart to your Angels and their love for you. Experience their support of your intentions to bring your Incarnate Self into harmony with your Authentic Soul. They are there!

Colors of the Four Worlds

Each World is vibrational energy and as such it can be represented by a color that matches its vibrational energy.

Atzilut is represented in the pure white Light. There is no differentiation in Atzilut, it is like the blank white paper that you stared into in the first chapter to get a concept of no differentiation, no depth, no comparison, for it is all one. This is like the sunlight as we "see" it outdoors. We actually don't see the sunlight, but we see it reflected off of the objects we are looking at in the color of their vibrational energy, a tree's green leaves, the red of the Earth, the clear blue of a tropical ocean. We see in the Sun's light, but we do not see the sunlight. Then, if you take a prism and put it in the sun the light is refracted (put into fractions of light) according to its vibrational energy. You see the rainbow in this "raying out" of sunlight. In much the same way, the World of Atzilut goes through filters (like the prism) and projects different Worlds, B'riyah into Yetzirah; Yetzirah into Assiyah – Spiritual Assiyah and Physical Assiyah. And each of these worlds carry their own color corresponding to the vibrational energy.

B'riyah is associated with the color blue. Even our language alludes to this, for how often do we say "It came to me out of the clear blue!" when we are speaking of an idea! Ideas are the reflection of Spirit in-spiring our thoughts, the connection of B'riyah, the World of Intellect linking Spiritual Assiyah, your mind. Blue is the vibrational energy color for B'riyah. The next world, projected out by B'riyah is Yetzirah, the World of Emotions.

Yetzirah is related to the color purple. Infinite Yetzirah connects to the heart of humanity to power up this Dimension, for our World of Emotions is our power plant. Have you noticed how many people are drawn to the color purple? Our world is being drawn together through global communications technology, and global economics, and yet, there are so many people who feel disconnected, isolated, and who are seeking love. Due to our ability and necessity to move and relocate we have gained a wonderful freedom but it comes with a price. To varying degrees some people have lost the sense of rooted-ness in a "village" and with it the sense of belonging to those people. Often the ties of belonging are now in the workplace, rather than the community, town or city. We still have plenty of emotions, but they need expression. The vibrational energy of the color purple brings expression of deep emotion, devotion, and spiritual belonging. No wonder we see it everywhere in our culture today! But, the color schematic between the worlds gets more interesting. The worlds continue to ray out another plane, the physical World of Assiyah, action! Knowing that the Hebrew for earth, soil, ground is *adamah*, because of the color of Mother Earth, what do you suppose the color of Assiyah is?

Assiyah is expressed in the vibrational energy of the color red. In Hebrew, *adamah* is the word for Earth, and from the same root, *adom* is the Hebrew name for red. What do you get when you mix blue (B'riyah) and red (Assiyah)? You have purple, the color of Yetzirah. This indicates the inter-dimensional aspects of the Four Worlds, for it is the power of Yetzirah that turns a thought (B'riyah) into an action (Assiyah).

These mystical teachings reaching down from Abraham became symbolically coded into the inspired writings of Moses in the Torah. Even the colors of the Four Worlds are found in the Sacred Ways given in the Torah.

What color is blood? Consider the wisdom in Leviticus 17 that tells us not to eat meat with the blood in it, for the Life of all flesh is in the blood. The blood carries the Life-force transformed into physical being within the blood cells. The Life-force is within oxygen, or ruah, breath, wind, and also spirit. Any region of the body that does not get free circulation of blood begins to die. The Life is in the blood. The blood is the color of Assiyah, the physical world.

These colors of the Four Worlds are used in the Mishkan, the sacred space of meeting with the Holy One in the Wilderness and later in the Temple in Jerusalem.

And you shall make for the Mishkan ten curtains of finely woven linen, and tekhelet, (deep blue), purple, and crimson yarns (deep red), with artistically made Angels you shall make them.
Exodus 26:1

Imagine what it would be like to go deeper and deeper into the Mishkan with the heightened ability to transcend with the energy of the colors surrounding you in the curtains which were the walls! As you enter the Sacred Space with your intentions to meet with the Holy One, and move from one room of curtains of crimson with Angels on them, signifying the World of Assiyah, to the next chamber with its curtains of purple with Angels on it, signifying the World of Yetzirah and on you would move even deeper into the Holy Place, transcending in your consciousness as you become surrounded with the color of deep blue, the color of the World of B'riyah. There your consciousness would move to its highest. The World of Atzilut was represented by the Holy of Holies, the chamber behind the veil where the Ark of the Covenant was kept. It was gold with two Angels facing each other touching the tips of their wings together on top of it. Within the Ark lay the stone tablets of Moses, Aaron's staff, and a jar of *manna*, the miraculous food that the Children of Israel ate in the Wilderness; it fell each night by grace from the Holy One. The High Priest would only enter the Holy of Holies and approach the Ark to make atonement once a year. It was such a Holy Place in the Luminous Presence that he wore bells on the hem of his garment so the other Priests outside the veil could hear him moving, and thereby tell that he was still alive. Atzilut is the place of Emanation, the Oneness; it is the place of The Source, and undifferentiation. The sacred meeting place of the Children of Israel in the Wilderness experience was built to exact instructions given by God and it enabled the worshiper to transcend to the Higher Dimensions.

We no longer have the Temple in Jerusalem, but we are able to bring our prayers and meditations in our Soul's vision into the Temple which resides in the Higher Dimensions, through the colors of crimson, purple, and deep blue, up through the very portals of Heaven.

The Four Worlds Represented in the Elements of this Dimension

In order to utilize the Four Worlds model in our rituals in this Dimension we use the four elements, Fire, Air, Water, and Earth. Rituals are intentional actions that effect a particular transfer of Divine Energy through the Higher Dimensions (by our intentions) and brings it into this World of Action. Each element holds symbolic meaning of characteristics of the Divine Energy in the Higher Dimensions. Each of the Four Worlds is thus represented through one of the four elements of this planet.

Atzilut, the World of Emanation is the place of the Ain Sof Or, the Endless Light. From Light comes the flame. **Fire is the element for Atzilut**.

B'riyah is the World of Thought. Just as we say an idea came out of the clear blue, we are referring to the Air, the skies over us. This represents the Higher Dimensions. **Air is the element for B'riyah**.

Yetzirah is the World of Emotions. Our emotions are in flow and flux, rise and fall, just as is water. Our emotions give birthing energy to our actions, just as the birthing waters of Life. **Water is the element for Yetzirah**.

Assiyah is the World of Actions, the physical world. It is easy to understand why Earth is the element that represents the physical world, for it is the physical world, infused with spirit, as PA is infused with SA. **Earth is the element for Assiyah.**

Whenever one of the elements is present in our Sacred History (stories in the Bible), the story is using symbolism to reveal a deeper understanding about one of the Four Worlds which is essential to the teaching of the story. For instance, the story of the flood and Noah uses water and teaches a great deal about how to "ride out our emotions" and how the same Life giving waters (emotions) can be destructive as emotions can also be.

Now that you are aware of the Four Worlds, the Infinite and the Finite, where are you in these worlds and where are these worlds in you?

Your Incarnate Self
The Manifestation of Your Authentic Soul

Your Authentic Soul is your Eternal Being which dwells in the Higher Dimensions. In the image of God, the Divine Emanator, it too emanates, **manifesting** itself as an Incarnate Self, who you know yourself to be in this Lifetime in the World of Assiyah, the physical world. Your Incarnate Self has two parts, both integrated and intrinsic to each other, to create you as a human being having the human experience. It manifests in your SA, Spiritual Assiyah, as the psyche, the mind and emotions, the transformer of spirit, to the World of Action through the PA, Physical Assiyah, which is your elemental body.

SA has within it SA B'riyah, Spiritual Assiyah B'riyah, your thoughts and SA Yetzirah, Spiritual Assiyah Yetzirah, your emotions. They are not the same as the Infinite B'riyah and Infinite Yetzirah, for they are finite, within the factors or time, space and Self. They are a chosen manifestation of your Authentic Soul for the purposes of the particular incarnation or Lifetime you are having. Without the agent of your elemental body there can be no action in the physical world and the energy falls short of being brought into this world. Your Authentic Soul desires to emanate by design. Remember, this is an extension of the Emanations of the Holy One. The unique features of your body, PA, mind and heart, SA, for each Lifetime will support and promote the fulfillment of that desire of your Authentic Soul. This becomes your "destiny" in that particular Lifetime.

We use the mind to "locate" the seat of SA B'riyah and the heart to "locate" SA Yetzirah. Your mind is not physical – your brain is, but your mind is Energy. Your heart refers to the seat of emotions, not to the physical blood pump in your chest. Your feelings are easily located emanating from the chest area. If you are extremely happy or in love you touch your chest in the heart area and it feels as if it will burst! If you are in the depths of grief there is even physical pain in the area of your heart. Your chest aches. It is very important to understand the difference between your thoughts, mind and your heart, feelings.

Very often I will ask someone, "How do you feel about that?" They will begin their answer, "Well, I think…" Then again I ask them, "But, what do you feel?" There are times in spiritual counseling when I will ask someone, "What do you think?" And they will start a reply with, "Well, I feel there is …" Those are your feelings, not your thoughts.

There is a difference between our thoughts and our feelings. There is a tremendous difference in the Infinite Worlds of B'riyah and Yetzirah! Have you ever tried to help someone out of their gloomy or depressed mood by explaining things or using logic? It won't work! Because they are focused on their SA Yetzirah and you are appealing to their SA B'riyah! They are in their heart and you are talking head! Have you ever been struggling with an issue in your Life and said, "I understand it in my head, but I just get stuck. I can't do it." That is because it has not traveled the longest distance in our body – from our head to our heart. Once you "get it" down in your heart the actions will come through easily, because our emotions are the power plant that brings our thoughts into the physical world of action. The key is to visualize (thereby doing it) opening a passageway from your head to the heart, then visualize opening your heart and **receive** what your head already knows; allow it to enter into your heart to dwell there and feel it!

We all experience times when we don't know exactly what is

wrong, but something has gotten on our nerves. Have you ever been "out of sorts" and when your loved one (usually carefully) asks you what is wrong you answer, "Nothing"? They can tell by your actions, your demeanor and, if they are sensitive, your energy, that something is upsetting you. They know something is wrong! And something is very wrong, but you may not be able to put your finger on any one thing or give them a reasonable explanation. How can you find out what is wrong and make an adjustment so you can "come back into your Light? There are two key words in the first sentence of this paragraph that give you a clue to the answer. You may not **know** what your problem is, but the word nerves indicates your **feelings** are the place to look for the message. The work of your nerves in your body is to send messages of sensations, your ability to feel.

If your loved one were to ask you, "Well, how does it feel?" Then, you might have plenty of answers! And those answers would lead you to your thoughts and together your thoughts and the feelings connected to them would give you the answer as to why "your knickers are in a twist." Voila!

The next time someone answers "Nothing" when you know something is bothering them, ask them, "How does it feel?" Try it out and see if it doesn't help them get in touch with what is wrong. A note of caution: be sensitive as to whether they are really ready to "talk" about whatever it is yet. Sometimes, we all need to process internally on an unconscious level before we are ready to open the door to our consciousness and face our conflict. If your friend is not ready to talk let them keep their silence in peace. You have opened a door for them and they may enter it within themselves before they are ready to go there externally. You can try this method with yourself as well. While it is easier with another person asking you the questions and listening to your answers it can work if you can internally play the dual roles of questioner and answerer!

Your thoughts and your feelings work in tandem, but they are different, serve unique purposes and they are worthy of individual exploration. The meditations in the last chapter will help you explore the worlds of your thoughts and feelings, SA B'riyah and SA Yetzirah.

Where is your Authentic Soul? Our human minds desire a location for the Authentic Soul to reside, in order to give relationship between it and our Incarnate Self, the chosen particulars of body, mind and emotions for a particular incarnation. However, Authentic Soul is a created being outside of "time and space." Therefore, it is Infinite, Eternal. It is of the Higher Dimensions. It carries differentiation, so it is beyond the Undifferentiated Oneness of Atzilut, but it emanates from it. It is in the first raying out of the Ain Sof Or, the Eternal Light, the Light of the Authentic Soul. It is in change and field. It is the early Light, exhale of God. That is the awe of your Authentic Soul.

How do you bridge the consciousness between your Incarnate Self and your Authentic Soul? To answer that question, consider the different layers of your consciousness. You have learned about Four Worlds. The Worlds of Atzilut, B'riyah and Yetzirah are Infinite Worlds. The World of Assiyah is both physical and spiritual. When you focus your mind only on the physical matter of this world it is as if the portals of your mind that lead you to the Higher Worlds close down. You still think and feel in your SA, however, they are the thoughts and feelings that are affected by your present incarnation and influenced only by your experiences in this Lifetime.

However, when you meditate or enter centered prayer or contemplative modes of thinking, you lift the veils or layers of consciousness and transcend through the open portals of your consciousness to move into the Higher Realms. You are not just **a** layer of consciousness, but layer-**s** of consciousness. It is from the state of expanded consciousness you can explore the consciousness of your Authentic Soul. This is done with the purpose of bringing the wisdom and light from that consciousness back into this world, into your SA and hopefully through your PA in your enlightened actions. The purpose of expanding your consciousness into the level of your Authentic Soul is to come into harmony with your Authentic Soul in this incarnate experience and to receive wisdom beyond your earthly experience. Then your SA and PA become tools and companions in the fulfillment of the Light of our Authentic Soul. This bridge of consciousness is sometimes called intuition. This word refers to an inner knowingness. Literally, this word means the inner tuition or inner teaching. It is the experience of going within your consciousness to transcend beyond your incarnate mind's knowledge. The more you familiarize yourself with the symbolic and forthright language of your intuition the more easily you will be able to access it. You will find words and information coming out of your mouth that you did not know a few moments before! I call this experience "when your Soul surprises your brain". Intuition is present within everyone. How much energy you put into developing it will determine your acuity in using it! You are accessing all the levels of your consciousness or levels of your Soul, for within the Kabbalistic teachings there are five levels of Soul, not all of which ever enter the World of Assiyah. You have within your Authentic Soul, five levels of Soul.

The five levels of Soul in descending order are *Yekhidah* (Oneness), *Khayah* (Life), *Neshamah* (Essence), *Ruah* (Spirit), *Nefesh* (basic Life – animation).

Understanding that we utilize different levels of our Soul for purposes of our destiny helps us to understand how all we have everything within us that we need to deal with Life! Remember, these levels of Soul are energy, and emanated from The One as The Many. They are as facets on a diamond, the sum of which creates the beauty of the whole.

Yekhidah is rooted in Atzilut, the World of Emanation. It is the Divine Potential. The word Yekhidah literally means "solitary, unique, only, alone, singular, stemming from the root word, *ekhad*, "one or someone". It is the potential of differentiality in concept. Concept is the blueprint.

Chayah is Life-force which is emanated out, the emanations or raying out of Life-force into actualization of differentiated energy. It is the exhale of the Creator.

Nashamah develops the "flavor", character and first essence of the Soul and is associated with B'riyah. You may have heard the word *neshumah*, in the Yiddish pronunciation. It is a wonderful juicy core, the deep essence of uniqueness. This is where you would come into a certain "field" with other Authentic Souls. Characteristics have developed that are unique and intrinsic to your Authentic Soul. "Uh, such a neshumah!" is a Jewish expression we use when we are describing a very sweet person whose actions come from the Soul. Neshamah can also mean breath, spirit, a living creature. From this we understand it is the highest of the levels that can move from the Authentic Soul to the Incarnate Self.

Ruah is the next level. Ruah is spirit, wind, breath, inspiration, but it is on a new level. It implies the movement of the energy. It empowers formation and is associated with Yetzirah, the emotions. The Ruah HaKodesh is the Holy Spirit of God. The words of the Prophets came forth when the Ruah HaKodesh was upon the Prophet. Just as the flow of Spirit from God empowers these words, so too, we have a level of Soul that is the flow of our empowerment, the forces of emotion. Even if we are not sure of the distinction of Ruah in our minds, our Soul does and we hear it in our colloquial phrases. A person or animal is "spirited". We refer to a spirit of sportsmanship, the spirit of giving at Christmas, and even fermented drink is called "spirits". If a spirited being is abused their spirit can be broken, a sad thing to witness indeed. This level of Ruah is usually present in varying degrees throughout Life.

Finally, **Nefesh** is the animation that gives movement to form which brings it into Assiyah, the World of Action. This word also means "breath". It is the Life-breath that gives existence in this world where everything must be in motion, or it transcends out of the Dimension. Every living member of Creation has the level of Nefesh within them. Have you ever been with a person when they died? Even if they were not conscious or non-responsive did you notice that once they quit breathing and the heart stopped there was something quite different about the body? The last level of Soul, Nefesh has left and it is as if it is no longer three dimensional. It takes on a stillness which seems beyond the cessation of heart and lungs. Even if it is the body of our loved one, there becomes something foreign about it. We honor the body and care for it in love, but something deep in our Soul tells us the one who looked at us through those eyes is not there. The eyes are empty and lack their Light. This is the beginning of the most difficult call to maturity of our love. For if our loved one gave us the opportunity to love in their Life, then in their death they can teach us how to truly live. To truly live means to live inter-dimensionally. The Light in our loved one's eyes is what continues to live, but it is not now reflected in a pair of eyes looking at us – for now it shines out through our own. As the physical drops away we must learn to transfer all of our emotions to the spiritual, continuing our love relationship with their Spiritual Being, their Soul. It is a most difficult transformation of our love, but the rewards of making that change has its rewards. For instance, our loved one is in Spirit or energy form outside of time and space. That means we can connect with their consciousness whenever we want to and enjoy their presence in our lives. While they were in human form they could only be in one place at a time, and we had to communicate by electronic technology or in person. Now they are as close as our very breath! This brings us back to the three levels of Soul which can incarnate, Neshamah, Ruah, and Nefesh – all three of which mean in some form, "breath", and symbolize the breath of God.

As human beings we have these levels of Soul within our Authentic Soul and Incarnate Self to the appropriate level for balance in our lives. The level of Soul within a person in a particular incarnation is not an indication of how enlightened or how much Light that Soul carries, because your AS may emanate an incarnation that would require that the higher levels of Soul were not present in your Incarnate Self, according to the demands of that incarnation's purposes. Each incarnation is unique; each pathway is different according to the "stage setting and backdrop" needed to play out the drama of that Lifetime. Human Beings are not the only Creatures with Soul. All of creation has levels of Soul in a way which brings balance and harmony.

For instance, Mother Earth has her higher levels in the Higher Dimensions that give potential and Life-force to and through the Four Worlds for existence in this World of Action, physicality. However, her Neshamah is in the essence of this planet, the "water planet" in our

Solar System. Water gives birth to Life. The waters of the Great Flood (Noah story) gave birth to the Earth as we know it. Her Ruah is the winds and currents that flutter across her face in the atmosphere, through her great waters and seas and through the movements of her platelets in her crust. Her magnetic field is her Nefesh, her animation. The magnetic field of Earth draws and repels, contracting and extending her forces around her globe and beyond her sphere. How much more so shall we care for Mother Earth with responsibility for our consumption and pollution of her as she is the Divine Life in physical form? We are one. It is all God. All of Creation is made of levels of Life-force, including you and me. We can draw upon these great levels to bring wholeness within ourselves and between us. You are not just a pretty face; the Light shining from your eyes is nothing less than the smile of God. Selah!

According to the Kabbalah, only the last three levels of Soul, Nefesh, Ruah, and Neshamah incarnate even among the most highly developed Souls and great leaders in spiritual transcendence. The two highest levels of Soul, Yechidah and Chayah, remain in the dimension of the Authentic Soul and are emanated constantly from Atzilut. A very highly developed Soul, one carrying a very bright light, brings in the Neshamah to a great degree. By degree, I mean that the consciousness and actions center on the leading of the Neshamah. The levels of Nefesh and Ruah are probably the most common levels to come into a Lifetime to reside and guide the Incarnate Self.

When I assist Souls who are in trauma, illness or who are transcending out of their Lifetime and returning to the Dimension of their Authentic Soul, I get very quiet and ask them what I can do to help their spiritual transition. When I have been with Alzheimer patients I have recognized that to the degree of the advancement of the illness, the levels of Soul have already transcended out of the person's Incarnate Self. Often, by the time family members are saying things to me such as, "This is not my mother. I wish you could have known her when she was herself" I realize that all of the levels of their Soul have gone out of this physical world except the Nefesh; the animation level is left. That is why the family and loved ones don't "recognize" them. When someone says, "This is not my father" I tell them, "Yes, it is. You are just used to interacting with them on a different level of their Soul. The part of their Soul from which they centered their consciousness and communicated in everyday Life is not what they are interacting with anymore.

From Souls who were in the transition process I have learned that we do have a number of days to fulfill in our Incarnation, and sometimes, while it seems a person is just there, not doing anything, not recognizing anyone, not creating, they are fulfilling their day, they are doing Soul work, they are staying in this Dimension until all their relationships are in order and they are finished here. They have taught me that Soul work may include gathering pieces or imprints of their energy that were stuck in certain places at certain times of their lives, especially when there was an impact of energy, such as physical trauma, emotional trauma, mental distress or spiritual wounding that has not been brought into healing (wholeness, balance). Many of the people with whom I have been with at their time of transition were alive during World War II and served in battle. Many soldiers endured physical, emotional and mental energy impacts of trauma from their war experiences. They have Soul work to do that involves gathering those pieces of their Soul that was left as an imprint in that situation and place. They sometimes do this consciously in Life review, but sometimes they do it in silence as they lie "unresponsive". They may be unresponsive to external physical stimulus, but their consciousness has shifted outside of time and space to gather its energy imprint back unto itself before leaving the body. When a society has rituals that do this work of healing the traumas of Life (such as war) the Soul work during the time of transition of the Soul is greatly eased.

Only in the Native American and ancient Hebrew spiritual practices have I found healing practices for the returning warriors in order to bring them back into peace. For Native American practices, see the book *Strong Hearts – Wounded Souls, Native American Veterans of the Viet Nam War*, by Dr Tom Holm, University of Texas Press. He is a professor at the Univiversity of Arizona. The Native American traditions recognize that one who has been on the path of war must re-enter the path of peace upon returning to the tribe, or the harmony of the tribe will be in jeopardy.

The purposes of wartime rituals in the ancient Hebrew traditions have a different focus, but a powerful purpose, none the less.

"When you take the sum of the Children of Israel, according to their number, then shall they give every man as atonement for his Soul unto the Holy One of Life.... Every one that passes among them that are numbered, from twenty years old and upward, shall give the offering (half shekel) of the Holy One...... The rich shall not give more, and the poor shall not give less, than the half shekel, when they give the offering of the Holy One to make atonement for your Souls.
Exodus 30: 12-15

In Exodus 30: 11-16, the numbering of the *anshei milkhamah*, warriors was accompanied with the giving of a half of Temple shekel. It was given as atonement for their Souls even before the event would occur. It was recognized that in war it was inevitable that they would take human Life, which must be atoned for by the act of giving, which is the opposite of taking. The amount was not the issue, therefore rich and poor gave the same, the Soul has no price; it was the act of Sacred Giving that was the ritual of power. The Hebrew word *cofer* which is used in this sacred text is used only three times in the Torah; each time referring to the shekel given by one who has taken human Life in circumstances that do not constitute murder. In this ritual it was impressed upon the warriors that regardless of the reason for battle, war was a necessary evil. The Sacred Way of recognizing the warrior's need for atonement for his Soul for the taking of Life even before there was a battle was linked to the need for a ritual to bring the warrior back to the tribe after battle.

And you (returning warriors) shall encamp outside of the Camp (of the Children of Israel) for seven days; whosoever has killed any person, and whosoever has touched any slain, purify yourselves on the third day and on the seventh day you and your captives.
Numbers 31:19

After returning from battle the warriors are given a set of instructions, Sacred Ways, to return to peace within the community of the Children of Israel. It was recognized that a ritual of transition needed to be made. The ritual of purifying themselves on the third and seventh days was T'vilah, immersion into *Mayim Chayyim*, living waters, (flowing water) completely covering themselves. The ritual of T'vilah is a transition ritual marking the change from one status before the immersion

to a higher status after arising from the birthing waters of Life It signified the necessity of rebirth into Life, washing away all that had
gone before and a desire to come back into harmony with Life (repen-
tance). This ritual enabled the returning warriors to release the ways
of war, body and Soul. Then and only then were they allowed back
into the Camp of the Children of Israel, into society. At all times, the
Sacred Ways addressed the need for spiritual integration of the physical, the need for wholeness, the inestimable value of the Soul, Life
and the need for harmony within and then between people.

In King Solomon's wisdom he avoided war through treaties, thereby expanding Israel to the largest economy, landmass and populous in
its history and teaching the higher way of harmony. It would serve our
countries well to learn the ways of King Solomon, to negotiate peace,
and to abolish war altogether. However, until that blessed time, those
who go to war have the need of rituals to successfully (harmoniously)
integrate their experiences into who they are and who they are to
become among the people, to give atonement for the lives they have
taken, and to bring their Souls back into rest and peace. This is eternal work, for it affects the Soul on all five levels.

Your Incarnate Self is made of integrated components of the PA,
physical body, the SA, the mind and heart (thoughts and feelings subject to the socialization and Life experience and the influence of the
chemical/hormonal balance of the body) and the infusion of various
levels of Soul in specific intensity. It is your choice where you focus
your consciousness. To bring all parts of your Being into balance,
integrating them harmoniously and adjusting them for each situation
you meet, is to aspire to maintain a state called *Shalom*. The root of
Shalom in Hebrew is *shalam*, which has the sense of completed, finished. For example, if I borrowed money from you and then paid you

back a portion at a time, when I pay back the last portion, it is "sha-lam" completed, whole, finished. Most people recognize the word Shalom to mean "hello", "goodbye" and "peace"; but it not only means peace, it is a blessing in greeting and leave taking of whole-ness. Shalom truly means the wholeness of harmony: that all of your Four Worlds, all your levels of Soul, are integrated in appropriate intensity and strength at any given moment to maintain harmony, wholeness, and Peace. When you bless another with words of Shalom it is a tremendous blessing indeed – it is to bless them with the state of wholeness, the experience of tranquility. Shalom!

Summary of the Four Worlds

Infinite World of Atzilut is undifferentiated Light, it is All One ray-ing out the Many. It emanates and projects Light into the World of B'riyah. It is represented by the element of **Fire**.

Infinite World of B'riyah is the Power of Intellect, thought, the first differentiation, random flashes of Light, the place of visions before words. The Light moves from B'riyah to the World of Yetzirah. It is represented by the element of **Air**.

Infinite World of Yetzirah, is the World of Feeling, emotions, a more dense energy, the place of lines connecting the dots, a place of connec-tions joining the points of Light to give it form. It is the place of rela-tionship. Yetzirah is the power plant which gives power to B'riyah's thoughts. It is feeling connected to thoughts to move to the Worlds of Assiyah, actions. It is represented by the element of **Water**.

World of Assiyah, is the World of Action in the physical world.

Assiyah is manifest in two parts in all of Creation:

Spiritual Assiyah
Thoughts (mind in a human)
Emotions (heart in a human)

Physical Assiyah – Physical World (body of a human)

It is represented by the element of **Earth**.

To be in a consciousness of Infinite Yetzirah and Infinite B'riyah you must shift your Incarnate Self consciousness. To be in SA consciousness is constant in this Dimension yet, you are not always conscious of your Spiritual Assiyah capabilities of transcendence. Your AS is constantly flowing Light down into your IS to fulfill your incarnation, but you are not always conscious of it.

When your emotions are out of sorts and you lose your peace of mind, it is an indication of a disharmony in the Higher Dimensions. It indicates your Authentic Soul is sending a message to you through your SA. If you do not recognize the message in your thoughts it will continue down into your emotions. If you still do not get the message it will continue into your PA and you might manifest the message as an illness or an accident. You experience the message in your body, because when your body is in disease, illness or accidental injury, all action stops. That brings the message fully into the World of Action, Assiyah. Your actions are stopped until you get the message! If the message is not heard or met the illness or injury may become chronic. All messages from the Higher Realm help you to make an adjustment in your Life for harmony.

As you learn to listen to your AS messages you begin to experience harmony between your Spiritual Assiyah and your Authentic Soul to a higher level. You begin to experience in your Life:

- Peace of mind – your SA B'riyah is connected to Infinite B'riyah
- Love, joy, contentment, and happiness your SA Yetzirah is connected to Infinite Yetzirah
- Health, flexibility – PA receives open flow of Divine Light from the Infinite B'riyah and Infinite Yetzirah through your balanced SA. Your body may even begin to "glow". Your countenance changes. Illnesses and injuries may go into remission or heal completely spontaneously. Your body becomes your comfortable "house".

All energy coming from Atzilut, undifferentiated wholeness, into B'riyah and Yetzirah are Infinite, yet move through the Dimensions to manifest in Assiyah, the World of Action – which is Finite. You are able to live your Life in peace and harmony, wholeness and to the highest of your intentions. You are a conduit for the Divine Light of the Holy One.

Journal Pages

Atzilut

The Hebrew word **Atzilut** means:

List the characteristics of the World of Atzilut:

What three factors pertain to Atzilut?

What created beings are essences of Atzilut?

What color represents the energy of Atzilut?

What element represents Atzilut?

B'riyah

B'riyah is Hebrew meaning:

List the characteristics of the World of B'riyah:

What three factors pertain to B'riyah?

What created beings are essences of B'riyah?

What color represents the energy of B'riyah?

What element represents B'riyah?

Yetzirah

Yetzirah is Hebrew meaning:

List the characteristics of Yetzirah:

What three factors pertain to Yetzirah?

What created beings are essences of Yetzirah?

What color represents the energy of Yetzirah?

What element represents Yetzirah?

Assiyah

Assiyah is Hebrew meaning:

List the two types of Assiyah:

List the characteristics of **Spiritual Assiyah**:

SA B'riyah:

SA Yetzirah:

List the characteristics of **Physical Assiyah**:

What three factors pertain to Assiyah?

What created beings are essences of Assiyah?

What color represents the energy of Assiyah?

What element represents Assiyah?

Five Levels of Soul

1. List the Five Levels of Soul.

1.

2.

3.

4.

5.

2. Which levels stay in your Authentic Soul?

3. Which levels are able to indwell your Incarnate Self?

4. List a key word for each level of Soul:

Example:

1. Yekhidah – Oneness

2. Chayah –

3. Neshamah –

4. Ruah –

5. Nefesh –

What is the difference between **SA B'riyah** and **Infinite B'riyah**?

What is the difference between **SA Yetzirah** and **Infinite Yetzirah**?

Where does your Authentic Soul "dwell"?

What World does your Incarnate Self live through?

What World are the Archangels created Beings from?

What World are the other Angelic Beings created in?

What World is Oneness, with no differentiation of Being?

Which World attracts you most? Why?

Notes

Chapter 3

Your Authentic Soul &
Your Incarnate Self

To thine own Self be true and it must follow, as the night the
day, thou canst not then be false to any man.
William Shakespeare

William Shakespeare, the English writer who shared his wisdom
through drama makes clear the case for being truly your Self in all of
your aspects, that you can enjoy Life in truth and share with others
your fullest humanity. In like manner God directed Abraham in the
words *Lech Lecha*.

The Divine Voice said, "Lech Lecha" which can literally be translated "Go to your Self". God instructed Abraham to leave the home of
his ancestors and go to a land that God would show him. It would be
a place of blessings for Abraham. This was an inaudible Voice of an
unseen God, telling Abraham to go to a place of which the location
was not revealed to him. It would be like hearing the Divine Voice tell
you "Take your family and get on I-95, and I'll tell you when to get
off – and there I will make a great nation of you"! This message came
to Abraham when he was already elderly with no children.

This was a Divine message to Abraham nearly four thousand years
ago, and yet these words from the Source of All Life echo down
through the hearts of all humans today. Go to your Self – therein lies
the breadcrumb trail which your Authentic Soul has left for you to
dwell in a place of peace and contentment, a place where you will

thrive, a place where what you do in this Lifetime will live on beyond you. All of your work which you contribute to the world and lives on beyond your Lifetime is symbolically spoken of as children. We are instructed to go "to Your Self" to find your destiny, to find your pathway, to find that which God will show you, go within, for that is where you find God. Within God is your destiny, your pathway. Your Incarnate Self finds its homeland within your Authentic Soul in he Higher Dimensions.

This is the Divine Voice encouraging you to go within your Being in order to go beyond your Being. Remember it is all God. When you go to your Authentic Soul you follow the trail leading back to The Source, your beginning and your destiny. Why would you do that, what is the effect?

Difference Between AS and IS

Your Authentic Soul (AS) leaves a breadcrumb trail for your Incarnate Self (IS) to follow to re-unite your consciousness between your Self and your Soul. This is not one instead of the other, but to include both to create more than one can be on its own. The Authentic Soul cannot affect the physical world without the Incarnate Self. The Incarnate Self is an emanation of the Authentic Soul, but it is not the entire consciousness of that Source. The Authentic Soul becomes the rooting and grounding in Infinite Resources, while the Incarnate Soul becomes the rooting and grounding in the World of Assiyah, the physical world of action.

In order to understand the Authentic Soul and the Incarnate Self it helps to know how we tell the difference between them. There are some exercises in your Journal which will also help you more deeply understand these unique aspects of your Being. Knowing these differences and aspects will help you when you are making decisions in your Life to stay true to your Authentic Soul and reflect your integrity through your actions.

Your Authentic Soul is an Eternal Being. It is Infinite. It changes by transforming in Light, vibrational energy toward its destiny and fulfillment in Atzilut. It is not locked in time or space. It is the Eternal Being that is you, that is not often explored by your Incarnate Self and yet is the part from which it is emanated and takes its Life-force. It is your portal to the Dimensions outside to time and space to the Infinite.

It does this by incarnating a part of itself that is necessary for fulfillment of the purposes of that incarnation. Your Authentic Soul has the power of intelligence and emotion, moving up toward Atzilut and yet reflecting downward toward Assiyah, as well. Your Authentic Soul births forth your Incarnate Self. This is how Spirit – pure energy – transforms into the physical world. The Holy One emanates Life in the Higher Dimensions, and continues the process of emanation as those Dimensions and the created energy in them continue to emanate out Life. Your Authentic Soul emanates your Incarnate Self, an aspect created and suited to the purposes of your Lifetime and Eternal development. I know my Incarnate Self as Victoria Hadassah Esther. But I know that this body and Lifetime will be finite, at some point my Soul levels will ascend back into my Authentic Soul. It too, is a birthing process. The process of returning home. Until that time, it is my role to truly live each day with the best of human dignity, in Eternal conversation with the Divine within me, my Authentic Soul, and the Divine Beings who guide me from the Higher Dimensions to fulfill my destiny and to give of the gifts I have to offer this world in joy. The Incarnate Self's Lifetime is also a process of refinement for the Authentic Soul, in that it is able to gain a higher level of Light through the challenges and exchanges of the events of that Lifetime. It carries this Light back into the Authentic Soul at the end of the Lifetime. During the Lifetime it is hopeful that the Incarnate Self will bring increasingly higher levels of Light (enlightenment) to the physical world in which it lives. One of the ways this is accomplished is through the Tikkun Olam, the repair of the world, acts which increase the quality of Life of others. Some of these are on the level of humanity and some are personal. An example of actions on the level of humanity is the discovery and development of Life-saving vaccines, such as small pox or penicillin. Diplomats who bring peace between warring nations, is also such an experience. Those who work for the preservation of the planet's resources, or for social equity for the oppressed are also involved in Tikkun Olam, the repair of the world.

Personal Tikkun work might be on a Soul level. If your Authentic Soul had a past incarnation that left an inequity between you and another person, you may meet them in another incarnation as a person in their own different incarnation and the drama between the two of you gives you both the opportunity to balance the energy and flow between you and even raise it to a higher level. This is often done unconsciously. However, there are many people who are "remembering" or opening to the hidden signals that they receive and understanding their connections with other Souls in their incarnation. It is important to balance the appropriate relationships for this present incarnation, while honoring the past connections of their Souls. This is quite often the case between family members and lovers. These are all purposes of an incarnation.

Your Incarnate Self is made up of your personality, character, roles you play in this incarnation, relationships you fulfill in this incarnation, gifts you bring to the world and the constitution and form of your

Elemental Body. It serves the purposes of the Authentic Soul in this Dimension for refinement of Soul, to bring Light to this Dimension and to fulfill contracts made with others before this incarnation. The body is considered as sacred as the Soul in the Kabbalah, because it is the means to bring Light into this Dimension. It is the love of The Holy One come into the physical world. It is considered Divine as the spark of God which dwells within it. This gives us a new way of relating to and honoring our body. In the chapter on meditations you will learn a meditation to help you build a positive and loving relationship with your body.

Some Soul contracts are made by the Soul (before coming into the world) to help others in their fulfillment, or for them to have an opportunity to help you. Contracts are made between parents and children, husbands and wives, sisters and brothers, grandparents and grandchildren.

Most often Soul contracts are reciprocal in nature. Both people help each other in some way. Sometimes you are able to balance karma or energy that your Soul is carrying which is out of balance for your Authentic Soul's harmony or the harmony of the physical Dimension. It may be energy held over from other Lifetimes and incarnations. These contract and purposes are expressed through the PA, in this Dimension. This is the act of manifestation. Even the moment of your birth is by design. Your Soul will move through the portals at the moment the energy is right for it to come into consciousness in this physical world. This is reflected in your astrological natal chart. The stars are given for times, seasons, and signs. Astrological information gives you indicators; it is a reflection of your strengths, weakness, challenges and gifts in your personal Life, your close relationships and your relationship to the world. It is a reflection of what has already been emanated by the Holy One of Creation **through** your Authentic Soul, into manifestation in physical form. The day that your Soul transcends back into your Authentic Soul, and your Incarnate Self is at rest, is also a day in fulfillment of your destiny by design. I learned while working in hospice that each Soul that I was with during their process of transcendence was by contract. I also learned that there was generally a person or persons who were by contract the ones to be there when they died. Sometimes there was a family member who wanted to be there when their loved one died. However, regardless of the vigil they kept at the bedside, their loved one waited until they were out of the room for one second, maybe just going to the bathroom quickly and that was the second they would transcend. It became clear to me that sometimes a person cannot leave as long as a certain person is in the room with them. It is as if they cannot let go of their loved one's energy in order to transcend. So they wait and die when the moment is right. So often the one whose vigil was fruitless blames themselves or is angry with their loved one. However, the deeper truth is they did not have a contract to be there and it all plays out in Divine Order. By leaving the room, if even only for a moment, they helped their loved one's passing. The challenge then becomes to re-establish their relationship in love, as it was in their Incarnate Self, with their Authentic Soul.

It is not by coincidence but by design that your Authentic Soul emanates your Incarnate Self to blend and fulfill the larger picture of all Creation – which is not whole without you and without which you are not whole.

Your body (PA) is a Being of the elements of this Dimension, a reflection of the Authentic Soul you are. It is a reflection, but is not your Authentic Soul.

When you are living this incarnation from the integrity of your Authentic Soul, you decorate your body, your home, your environment and your activities accordingly. You move away from the action of "shoulds" to actions from your choice of authenticity in Love. Your body will also change over time physically, reflecting the harmony of your inner Being. You will begin to live more and more fully and consciously.

At some point in time your Incarnation will be finished; your Soul will transcend, your body will return to the elements of the planet. Your SA B'riyah, thoughts and your SA Yetzirah, feelings will stop as well. Those parts of your psyche which have been shaped and restricted by time and space, the experiences of your Life, the socialization processes and your bodily affects will no longer challenge your Soul.

Remember I said your Soul transcends! All of the Light that you carry in your Soul continues on in your Authentic Soul consciousness outside of time and space. Your Soul will carry a higher level of Light when you transcend out than when you came into this Lifetime, because of all of the challenges you have met, what your Soul has learned, the Soul contracts you have fulfilled to help others and the struggles you have endured with dignity. Any karma or disharmony you have been a part of will be dealt with in the incarnation review outside of time and space after you die. You will be able to "see" then with a higher Light and more fully understand the mysteries of your Lifetime.

The Kabbalists say the Soul experiences what they call "The Sifting" for it sifts out those experiences and interactions in your Lifetime which are unfinished or are in need of repair. Your Soul, they say, will have an opportunity to do or contract to do *Tikkun Neshamah*, the Repair of the Soul – both yours and others whom you have impacted by the actions of your incarnation. During The Sifting the Soul integrates those experiences of learning of the Lifetime which are new or renewed for the Authentic Soul. All is for the purpose of gaining higher and higher Light, to eventually move the Soul back into the undifferentiated Oneness of The Source. If this idea seems rather frightening to you – to not exist in some form, then that is an indication that your Authentic Soul is not finished yet! You still have purposes and destiny to fulfill in the Infinite Worlds, for when a Soul is ready to transcend The Abyss to undifferentiated Being it is ready and moves with ease, compelled by the forces of Love, as two lovers merging in Divine Union.

Will you recognize loved ones in the Higher Dimension? Of course – but you no longer are restricted to relating to them in the physical; you are now free to see their Light and connect to their hearts through the love you share. Your love is the bridge that crosses the dimensions and links you eternally. In Shir HaShirim, the Song of Songs, Wisdom teaches us that "Love is strong as death". We know the love we shared and share continues Infinitely, Eternally. Very often when I have been with people as they transition out of their incarnation, loved ones who have already died come to be with them. They always recognize their loved ones. Sometimes a person might tell me that their mother or father, husband or wife came to them in a dream. There is never a question as to who it is. One lady who was a hospice patient told me that every night her husband (deceased) comes to her and she really wants to go to him, but he told her she is not allowed until he stretches out his hand to her. Then she can go. Soul recognizes Soul.

Souls in the Higher Dimensions are not limited to form as we are in the physical world of time and space. Therefore, there can be a transformation of energy to appear in a way that is recognized by the person in human form. When I am channeling a message from a loved one who has died to someone they will often appear in a form that as I describe it to the person to whom the message is intended they recognize the person from their Incarnate Self, even though their Soul is now out of Incarnation. For instance, I once described a young man who was very near to a young girl. His energy was coming through with the word romantic on it. As I described it she said that is her fiancé who had committed suicide three months before. He explained what had happened and why he did what he did on a spiritual level. His words have given her meaning to an otherwise senseless tragedy in her Life. He spoke to comfort her and help her realize he is there with her in spirit and to incorporate this event into her Life, but most importantly to keep on living Life. Our relationships are inter-dimensional when we open our Incarnate Self to experience the Authentic Soul levels.

You have never been in this Dimension as who you are in this incarnation before. There has never been a you as you are now before. There never will be again. This is the only time you will incarnate as the person you are. The world will never again have the "you" of this Lifetime in it. If future incarnations are emanated by your Authentic Soul you will have a different personality, character, social and cultural surrounding. You will have a different name. Your essence emanating from your AS will be different according to the mission of that new incarnation. You, just as you are today, are unique. This is a unique moment in the history of this Dimension for your presence as you are.

Getting To Know Your Authentic Soul and Your Incarnate Self

Knowing what is authentic to our Authentic Soul is often revealed in our lives as children. When a child is "fresh from God" the honesty with which he or she acts and chooses is profound. What did you especially like as a child? In your Journal you will notice that you are to star those likes that you list which showed up in your childhood. They often have important messages to us that can become obscured in the process of growing up, especially when we try to please those whom we love or when we try to impress someone important to us. Have you ever gone back to one of your favorite childhood activities and found that it still holds magic for you? Have you been on a swing lately and tried to go higher and higher? When did you last go on an "explore"? It could be as minute as journeying into the intricacies of a flower in your backyard or as grand as the adventure of hiking a mountain trail, continuing just around the next bend to see what is there, then the next, then the next... These activities that brought you joy as a child hold important messages about your Authentic Soul for you to hear, heed and integrate into your consciousness.

It is said that the little dip on the upper lip beneath your nose is where an Angel touched you so you would forget the Higher Dimensions and all you have known before and be able to focus on the current Lifetime you are entering. Even so, when a child comes into the world they are often still able to connect with and have dialogue with the animals, trees, grass and elemental energies. Their dream Life is often rich with meaningful dreams. If a past incarnation is being processed, finished or woven into the current Lifetime the child's dreams (even nightmares and night terrors) may be the place of that integration. It is important to remember your recurring dreams of childhood, or listen to the dreams of your children to gain the messages those dreams hold. We are seeing the Souls of children coming into the world with even more consciousness now than ever. It is a great benefit to the child whose parents teach him or her how to develop their intuition and spiritual guidance and transcendence, rather than dismiss it as "imagination." How many children do you suppose had an "imaginary friend" who they were told did not exist, when actually they were conversing with their Guardian Angel or Spiritual Guides or a transcended Master? A dream may be given to help a child learn not to be frightened by coming into the world again. They may have had a dangerous or frightening experience in the world before. The world is not the same, the buildings are not the same, people who were known before are now strangers who seem familiar, but are different. It helps to love and support your child or your inner child through the orientation and integration of sacred memory and current experiences. Won't it be wonderful when our schools teach children to develop their intuitive powers as well as learn the ABCs and math and reading? That will be an awesome world. Imagine the adults who will grow from those children! In the Journal Pages of this chapter you will be instructed to write down things of this world that you prefer and remember a preference for even from childhood. Those parts of your Self are deeply important to your destiny and Soul's purpose in this incarnation. That is why you will be using them in the exercises. You may feel you already know your preferences; however, writing them down helps you look at them outside of your Self. What things were your favorite childhood activities? What was magic for you? What held your imagination? What was the focus of your teenage years? There is a great country Western song about a young man who was on a wild date with a young lady. They were staying out late, her father peppered the tailgate of his pick-up truck with a shot gun and throughout the chorus of the song the young man sings, "I know what I was feeling, but what was I thinking, what was I thinking, what was I thinking?" In childhood physical growth is our focus. In our teen years we are focused on emotional growth, making bonding relationships with those outside of our parents. What occupied your young adult years? By then we are usually focused in our mental development, the gathering of knowledge for our Life's work. If you are old enough, what was the focus of your mid-Life and elder years? Our spiritual growth becomes the focus as we seek to find the deeper meaning to Life. Instead of giving physical birth to children we begin to give spiritual birth to others as we share our wisdom. Through our incarnation we are uniting and integrating the Four Worlds within us and beyond us. This process is taking less and less time in our generations. Today, many young people are focused upon the deeper meaning and higher work of healing and gifting the world with their talents and gifts at a younger age.

Consider this question. Have you ever met someone you know that you do not know, yet there is something that you recognize and embrace? You just have an immediate sense of friendship and connection. This is called Soul recognition. You may know this other person from other incarnations and often do. You may know this person from the Higher Dimensions and the interaction of your Authentic Souls. Sometimes this intimacy can become confusing in that the other person is in a different Lifetime and will not always respond to you in the way of a previous Lifetime. Sometimes you may have intimate feelings for this person which would disrupt their Life and yours if you acted upon them. It is important for you to recognize what you are feeling as well as where those feelings are coming from. What you do with those feelings can have a profound affect on both your and their lives. This is why it is so very helpful to remain grounded, to know, understand and honor your Self well, and to stay true to your Self and your highest intentions for your Self while you venture through the mystery of your current incarnation.

When we come into this world as babies we are still "fresh from God" and the full of the experience of our Authentic Soul consciousness. The processes, goals, issues, challenges and contracts of our lives lay before us to fulfill through the destiny of our Incarnate Self. These incarnation purposes often begin to reveal themselves to our conscious mind arising from our unconscious senses throughout our early childhood. Quite often the themes of the purposes of our destiny are aligned with the themes of our favorite fairy tales and childhood stories. As children we are still quite open to an exchange of communications with animals, "inanimate objects" and "invisible beings". We also connect with the mythical and fantasy characters of storybooks and fairytales, for on a deep level, we still "remember". Retaining and developing this "knowing" is the honor and responsibility of parents and teachers, in order for children to grow in their wisdom gifts and their inner guidance. As adults we can recapture some of what we "knew" about our Authentic Soul's intentions for our Incarnate Self by exploring our memory of early childhood experiences. Your Journey Book will provide an exercise for you to interpret your favorite childhood fairy tale for insight into this Lifetime.

When have you sat watching a spider make her web, or simply sat quietly to feel the energy of the Earth around you? These times are important to your Incarnate Self to gain Light from your Authentic Soul and integrate it here.

The Kabbalah says if you are seeking an answer to a question, take a journey and you will find the answer on your journey. This is because you have changed all that is familiar to you, you become more aware of your surroundings and you are active, moving forward. This action calls forth from the Higher Dimensions within you a "moving forward" on your pathway within, thereby finding the answer to your questions. You are expanding your awareness in the world by the new experience. As you integrate the new around you there is an expansion of your framework within as well. You become open to receive – and thereby receive the answers to your question.

What was your favorite childhood fairytale? What childhood stories did you ask to hear over and over? Did you have a favorite Bible story or character from the Bible? What was the theme of each story? The theme gives you a hint as to the message your Authentic Soul was giving your Incarnate Self in childhood to guide you in your destiny, your incarnation pathway. In the Journal pages of this chapter you will have an opportunity to explore your favorite stories and what their messages are for you.

Just as your mind is working in concert with your body's intelligence, so your Authentic Soul is working in concert with your Incarnate Self, through your SA B'riyah, your mind. It may be unconscious, but how much more beneficial to be conscious of this process and messages? The more attuned you are to you're AS, the sooner you realize the message.

Your Authentic Soul Guides Your Incarnate Self

Your Authentic Soul intrinsically connected, sends messages through your Spiritual Assiyah and your Physical Assiyah, if necessary, to move your Incarnate Self into action for harmony within your Life.

But how do you access your Authentic Soul? In the first chapter on

Differentiation I mentioned that one of the tools to access the infinite resource in your Being is your imagination. Imagination is just putting an image to that which is formless from the Higher Dimensions. Imagination in Hebrew is *dimiyon*, from the root, *d'mu'i*, comparison, simile. This does not indicate that the imagination is not real, only that it is similar. It has been said that "Imagination is our memory of the future." This is understood as the flow of thought energy that comes from our Authentic Soul which is outside of time and space to our Incarnate Self in time and space to "imagine" or put an image or vision to that which is still future in this Dimension. This is the creative process. This is how a musician "hears" the music of a composition, new to this world, but which exists in the Higher Realms. Imagination is one of the tools we use to access the "program", the immeasurable treasure of your infinite resources within you. When you travel outside of time and space, receive (Kabbalah) the inspiration and then come back with that inspiration, you are "remembering the future". It gives a new meaning to "back to the future." The tool of imagination is so important to nurture in our children! When you use meditation or visual or guided imagery you are opening the portal to the Higher Dimensions, that you may access the Infinite, setting your intention to bring Light back with you.

Another way of accessing the Authentic Soul within you is through your interactions with others. We each serve to call forth from within one another that which we cannot see within ourselves. How can you grow in faith through your interaction with another person? While you cannot apply faith to others from the outside, you can call it forth from within them by your own faith. You have faith (all you need to deal with Life) within you. For example, a couple, both licensed realtors, wanted to start their own Real Estate company. It was quite ambitious and the wife said it wasn't possible. The husband believed they could. Why not? Then, going on his faith, he talked to her about it and he began to tell her what was possible with quite inspiring words. As she listened she began to think and feel that it was possible – maybe the two of them could do this! In the ensuing months their business began to grow. The more they worked as a team the more successful the company grew. He could not apply his faith to her from the outside, but he called forth from within her that which was there to start with. She just needed access to it! You can reach into the Dimensions of your AS beyond the proof of the "seen" in this physical world, to hold your faith, your belief in the unseen within your Incarnate Self. You can help others to become – actualize – that which they have been created to be. However, the same holds true for you. Others can call forth from within you that which you do not see within yourself to become everything you have been created to be. It is called forth from within your A.S. As Father Cornelius van der Poel says, "In this we become co-creators with God." You are who you are because of others in your Life, and your loved ones are who they are because of you in their lives. In this as long as you exist, you cannot be separated!

Nothing of spirit can be expressed in this world without the body. **Any effect that your thoughts and feelings are going to have in this world must be expressed through the body in an action or word.** Think about that for a moment! Your body is the key element. And element it is, for it is made of molecules matching the elements of the physical world.

Your Spiritual Assiyah is the first transformer of the energy of the inspired messages from your Authentic Soul and Beings of the Higher Dimension. They come in the form of inspired and creative ideas. Then the energy drops into the area of your Incarnate Self's emotions.

Finally, those ideas and emotions find action through your body in word or deed. This is how God, the Angels, Divine Guides, Ascended Masters, Holy Spirit (Ruach HaKodesh), and Shekinah (the feminine aspect of God in the physical world) intervene and act in this world through you. It must come through your body; your magnificent and wondrous body. There are no actions that are not driven by thoughts and emotions, even if they are unconsciously connected. Everything done in this world begins as a thought and an attached feeling within someone. Beautiful music begins as an inspired vibrational energy (high or low). It goes through the transformer of the mind of the musician, and it attaches to his or her emotions that give it expression through the written music or an instrument. Art, healing, politics, teaching, service to others, any action you can name, whether it promotes Life or diminishes Life, all comes through this transformative process. Even if you are not consciously guiding what comes out of your mouth, your words will come as the flow from what is in your mind and heart.

Your SA and PA can be affected by what you eat, whether you are rested, your environment, what you wear, and the temporal conditions surrounding you in your Life. How can what you wear affect you? Have you heard the saying, "The clothes make the man"? In reality, what you wear has a vibrational energy in the fabric and in its color. That affects you. When you purposefully choose that color and fabric it reflects what is going on consciously inside of you, even what mood you are in. Your Authentic Soul is not affected; it is outside of time and space. However, your ability to express your Authentic Soul through your Incarnate Self may be affected. When you are not purposefully choosing your clothes they will reflect what you are unconsciously feeling and thinking inside! How do you feel when you are wearing silk, light as gossamer? How different do you feel in denim? How might you express your inner being differently in denim than silk? Everything affects your Incarnate Self, and therefore can affect the relationship (connection) to your Authentic Soul. It is important, therefore, to be aware of what is affecting your Incarnate Self and your ability to express your Authentic Soul.

You are vibrating at a particular rate. Everything in existence is carrying its own vibrational energy and rate. When you encounter that which is vibrating at a rate harmonious to you it is a pleasant sensation, an easy fit. Your dislikes are those things which are not in harmony with your vibration. They do not resonate with you. When you learn what things are in harmony with you then you can surround yourself with that which heightens your vibrations and let go of that which does not resonate with you without guilt. In your Journal are exercises that will help you explore your Incarnate Self as you know it. It will lead you on your bread crumb trail back to your Authentic Soul. Knowing these unique aspects of your Being will help you to stay true to your Authentic Soul when you are making decisions in your Life. Being in harmony with your Authentic Soul is your Path of Peace. Your intuition is that transcendent pathway between your SA mind and feelings and the Higher Dimensions and your Authentic Soul to help you stay true to your Authentic Souls purpose in this Lifetime.

Your intuition is the state of consciousness beyond the veiling of the World of Assiyah, which gives you access to a higher wisdom and knowingness. It is the ability to access your Higher Levels of Soul outside of time and space. When you learn to trust your intuition you learn to trust your own Soul. Then your AS can communicate more clearly and purposefully with your IS. Your intuition is at work when you have the experience of speaking information that is new knowledge even to you. For instance, have you ever had the experience while teaching well-known material you have prepared, that you suddenly began to bring forth wisdoms and more information that you yourself knew or prepared? It is as if your Soul surprises your brain. It is as if someone behind you said it using your mouth! You have tapped into the flow of your intuition (inner teaching) and are channeling the information through from the Higher Dimensions.

While your AS is emanating each Lifetime you experience, not all Lifetimes contain the same purposes, so you have different aspects of your totality of Being for support in any particular Lifetime. Sometimes you have gifts, characteristics or strengths in other Lifetimes, which are shut down in your current Lifetime. Sometimes the challenges of the incarnation would not play out according to Divine Purpose if those gifts were in play. Have you ever sensed that you have a skill on the inside – maybe playing a certain musical instrument – but in this Lifetime you struggle to learn to play it? This is why sometimes something may seem familiar to you, however, it is denied you in this Lifetime. Have you ever been in a foreign country, and you felt like you should be able to just rattle on in the language of that country, and yet your mouth has difficulty forming the words? Have you experienced knowing what something says in another language that you have not studied before? These are indicators of past lives lived in places using those languages. I have also known people who are more comfortable with the ancient form of a language than the modern form, such as Old French, and Old English. The language of Shakespeare is nearly unintelligible as the same basic language of English when you compare it to American English spoken in New York or Atlanta, Georgia.

Your comfort levels are hints as to past lives spent expressing yourself in another way. As well, I know people who are not comfortable trying to use the spoken word as a language for communicating thoughts at all! This is an indication your Soul is used to communications in other energy transfers in other Dimensions. Stick with it – you will learn how to use words! They are power in this World of Assiyah!

As a very young child, my son had a habit of speaking in French and other languages when he was asleep. He also did not learn to speak as quickly as his sister, even so he became an avid reader and uses vocabulary with a sharp wit. He is the only person I know who can *tell* a cartoon. A cartoon is a visual and usually you must see the picture to get the humor. He can translate visuals into language in such a way as to carry the visual humor with it.

Our Authentic Souls do not all "reside" in the same Dimension. They are seeded in myriads of Dimensions beyond our knowing – but your Incarnate Self can know. As you learn to communicate with your AS you will find you do not need words in the deepest communications. There is a transference to your IS that does not take time and is beyond your IS experience; and it may take some time to think through that which only took a nanosecond to "download" from your AS!

Choosing your actions in Life from your Authentic Soul means doing what you love everyday for the rest of your Life. Follow me on this now. When you are doing what you love it has the reciprocal effect of you truly experiencing joy for being you. When you enjoy being you then you begin appreciating your own awesome existence in all your uniqueness, not because of what you do, but because you exist. When you experience this sense of awe in the fact of your Being, you are content to BE – what ever you BE. You illumine your consciousness to include Being God's Love made manifest in this Dimension and beyond to Eternal Dimensions. You can choose every-day for the rest of this incarnation to love and yet there is more – **you are Love**. You don't need to fill your Life with Love from the outside, for you are Love. Divine Love is what you are made of, it is your Life-force. It fills you to overflowing from within you and splashes over onto others. You need not struggle to become anything or anyone else; just BE. Your choices come from within you. You can say, "I love being me!" And that thought gives way to feelings of contentment.

Sometimes, however, even when you are surrounded by the best situation for your harmony you may feel "out of sorts." When your thoughts and feelings are out of harmony with your AS you might feel agitation, discontent, irritable. Your thoughts may be confused, out of focus, out of order. You may have that little "nudgy" thought that just won't go away. Your Authentic Soul will send messages to you which manifest as a lack of peace of mind and displaces your emotions. When something happens that makes you angry you may respond with anger beyond what is warranted by what happened. This is an indica-tion that your AS has sent a message to your IS that is in your mind and emotions, but has not yet been consciously acknowledged. If you ignore the message and do not take time to understand the symbolic language of your mind and emotions the messages will drop down to the next level, your physical body. Sleep may evade you, or you may contract an illness or have an accident. These can all be means by which your Authentic Soul is sending you a message. The more sen-sitive you become to the harmony within your Incarnate Self the more readily you will receive the messages in their subtle stage rather than the "two by four" when it gets to the physical stage. The severity of the body message is relational to the degree of your inharmonic state with your Authentic Soul.

What kind of illness or accident, where it is located in your body, and what body systems are affected are all symbolic language used by your AS to give you information about something that is causing disharmony in your IS and your Life that you are not conscious about or are choosing to ignore. Louis Hay in *You Can Heal Your Life,* has done seminal work to help you unlock the mystery of the symbolic language of your body in illnesses and injuries.

Begin to notice what injuries you seem to receive repeatedly in your Life. Whether we are injured on the right or on the left, in the front or back are all meaningful to the message. This is not to lay blame, but to help you realize how the Universe and your Authentic Soul, and God, ultimately, are constantly supporting you toward prosperity of health. These messages in illness or accident have nothing to do with punishment or judgment, but are a means by which you can hear deeper and see farther than the apparent veil of the physical world. What illnesses did you have in your childhood? What illnesses do you seem to be plagued with repeatedly throughout your Life? Is there a particular body system that is especially vulnerable? What is your most common complaint at this time in your Life? These are all clues to messages being sent by your Authentic Soul to restore harmony in your Life.

Let us take the common cold for an example. Who has not experienced this most inconvenient illness? If Life cannot get your attention any other way physical discomfort works every time! But, what is the message? You tend to run to the medicine cabinet for all of the remedies and symptom relievers. But, the message is in those very symptoms, so while you wait for your Airborne to fizz away, make a list of your symptoms and begin to interpret their messages according to

what is going on in your Life. Start asking yourself some questions
such as:

- What is most uncomfortable?
- When was the onset?
- What has been going on prior to or around that time?
- How are my eyes?
- How are my ears?
- How are my sinuses?
- How is my throat?
- How are my lungs?
- Am I coughing?
- Do I have a temperature?

You get the idea! The answers to these questions will give you a hint
as to the message you are receiving through your PA. The sooner you
get the message and take action to rectify the imbalance that it is
pointing to in your Life the sooner those colds remedies are going to
work! Try it! Even though we can find the biological root cause of an
illness, it still carries with it messages. These messages are answered
not instead of medical attention, but in tandem with medical attention.
Why? Because you are not just a physical body, but you are also a
spiritual being. Both must be addressed in order to receive a *refuah
sheleimah*, a complete healing, body, mind and heart. The inner messages manifested in the physical body are making you as sick as the
manifestation itself. The cold is not the illness; it is a symptom. It is a
symptom that your SA is out of balance somewhere. When illnesses
such as colds strike it tells us our immune system is compromised in
some way. Yes, and that is the message that your psycho-social spiri-

tual balance has gone haywire. So, take care of the cold, and heal the inner being, saying a little prayer of thanks to your Authentic Soul who, in love, has sent you this message for your healing.

A cold is systemic, so that tells you there is a systemic imbalance going on. It often affects the sinuses which speak of your means of bringing in Life-sustaining breath, symbolic of spirit, and feminine energy. In fact the same word for breath, ruach, also means spirit in Hebrew. Are you having difficulty with a feminine energy in your Life? Is everything clear or stopped up with your Mother or Daughter?

Is your throat on fire? Symbolically your throat is your power center and center for creativity through your voice. What is your Soul on fire to say? You use your breath moving through your vocal cords to create vibrations that you then form into vibrational sounds in your mouth with your tongue, which creates change in the world around you. That's a lot of power! Your throat is also the passageway between your head and your heart. Is your throat constricted, swollen? Are you constricted when you try to move from your thoughts to your feelings right now? Your throat area is the place of knowledge when you balance your thoughts with empowerment from your heart. It is also the passageway for your food and drink to go to the stomach to be digested and send nourishment to the body. Are you constricting your nourishment? Is the nourishment you are giving yourself burning you or easy to swallow? Is Life hard to swallow right now? Are angry words stuck in your throat?

Colds can also be accompanied by a cough, or an attempt to clear the throat symbolic of an attempt to be heard. Coughs also clear the lungs, the place that sends Life-giving oxygen to the body. That is the place of exhortation. When we are vibrating at a high level of joy we exhort others, and spread the joy and love, raising their vibrational energy as well. During a cold our muscles may feel achy and stiff. Our ability to move is limited by discomfort. All of these messages (and often more) are in a little cold.

When a cold comes into your Life you can ask yourself:

- Do you have a cough? Are you not being heard or trying to be heard (voice and throat) in Life? Are you barking to get someone to hear your words? (This often happens to children who are not being heard.)
- Are you not giving yourself the nourishment you desire; are you giving yourself food for growth and bringing in the sweetness of Life? (Also a major message for Diabetes, by the way, Sweetie).
- Are you filling your Life with joy, doing fun things? (lungs)
- Are you giving your body the time off from the busy-ness of Life regularly so you can integrate the events of your Life?

What is the best medicine for a cold? I know everyone has their favorite symptom "band aid" and favorite liquids to help keep the body hydrated, but what is your body really giving you the message about? Remember, this is a message from your Authentic Soul. It is speaking to you about deeper matters than just getting to bed a little earlier. What is the best way to help your body recover from a cold? Rest. True rest. Staying in bed and sleeping your head off kind of rest. If you are just taking work home and doing it there, balancing caring for children, cooking, or doing "home chores" that is not taking it easy and you are helping yourself to a few extra days or weeks of having a cold! The message your sore muscles are giving you is "I don't want you to move." That's not hard to understand. The "time-out cold" can give you the opportunity to let the dust settle in your Life long enough to see with clarity and adjust your priorities to come back in harmony with your highest good. It is a time to move back to your integrity and live what is authentically you. It is a time to eliminate activities that do not serve your highest purpose. Your Authentic Soul will tell you these messages in your mind – you know when you are not feeding yourself spiritually as well as physically and when your Life is out of balance. But it is easier to ignore the mental nudges. Your AS will use your emotions by your feelings of grumpiness, anxiety or despair and depression over "not enough time" issues. Ignoring these messages tends to only compound the inner discord. Remember, your emotions are your power plant. You are playing with dynamite now! Finally, your body says, "Okay, enough. So you won't stop? We will help you out." Bam! You begin the coughing, sneezing, headachy syndrome. Sound dismal? It is all in support of you. Not your husband, partner, wife, not your children, not your mentor or teacher. You. You are important enough for all that effort from your AS, just because you are. Just because you exist. Your Incarnate Self is the seat of action for your Authentic Soul in this Dimension. Your AS will give you messages to help you stay in tune. You are not alone. You are an intrinsic part of The Whole. The Whole supports you as it is supporting itself in evolution to the Light.

You can also read what is happening to humanity in the world by the ills of society in general. There for a while children were all having their adenoids and tonsils removed. Then there was a generation of women who were having hysterectomies right and left. Then there was a rise in open heart surgery. Now, migraine headaches, acid reflux and diabetes seem to be on the rise to the point of epidemic. I will resist the temptation to address the ED scene here. As you can see, your PA will give you every opportunity to bring your Life back into balance.

I found it interesting while I worked in hospice to compare the functioning of the individual with a terminal illness with what I saw going on in their lives: how they related to themselves, to others, to The Infinite Creator, God. In most instances I could see a correlation between the dis-function of the patient and their family system and the messages that the terminal dis-ease represented. For instance, many cancer patients had something that was "eating them" that was a stress in their lives that they had not faced and addressed, but had allowed to fester within them, most often in the area of their lives represented by the system affected. Many heart patients have emotional issues they have not been able to resolve. These are not hard and fast rules, however, for the art of the Soul's purposes are multi-faceted and Mystery! We do not judge, but support.

Are you suffering with headaches? How many times do you take headache remedy meds? The next time you feel a headache ask yourself what you are feeling guilty or fussing at your Self about on the inside. The headaches are saying you are beating your Self up mentally or beating your head (thoughts) against a wall.

I saw a commercial for a diet aid. It was true headache material. The lady was dancing around saying, "I am so excited! I went from a size 10 to a size 4!" Anyone else feel animosity toward this innocent child? I would be very happy with a size 10 today! Any woman who has been through child bearing, menopause and her second Saturn Return knows the value of good comfort food! But what are you doing with the "guilt" that it brings? The headaches are IMs. They are Instant Messages asking you to take some time to look at your attitudes and how you are NOT treating your Self in love. They ask you to sort through your "shoulds" and keep the helpful ones, doing something about them, and let go of the fake ones (ones that do not truly reflect your integrity or the highest intentions for yourself). Do you need to shed a few pounds for health reasons (not because society says you are suppose to look like Charles Atlas with size 34DDD b'zooms added on for good measure)? Then the first thing you must do is to begin a program of loving your body; for true healing, harmony and balance come only through love. The headaches begin to fade. Your body will tell you at what weight and toning it feels comfortable. You will find the meditations on the PA in the last chapter helpful with your body relationships.

Now you know that the incidents in your Life all have meaning for you. You have a means by which to read the signs toward the truth and integrity, and the pathway of peace of your Authentic Soul. You are the best interpreter of these messages. Sometimes you might find it helpful to talk with someone who understands physical body messages if you are blocked by your own emotions. Other times, it might help to have one of those "screaming mimi's" moments with God. Let it out, God and the Universe will not fall apart from your outpouring, but you will release the energy that can block your own hearing of the Still Small Voice. In the moments of exhaustion after such a moment you are likely to hear the simple truth, the "Aha!" you were looking for. The more you shift your consciousness to center in your Authentic Soul, the more your Incarnate Self experiences peace of mind, and a fullness of heart. The more you remain in this consciousness the more your body takes on a brighter health and balance. Your body will begin to manifest the strength of your inner flow of energy from and to your Authentic Soul. It will come into a glowing state of health.

Your AS is not affected by the conditions of your Incarnate Self. It remains steady. It is your place of Serenity, your center for Clarity. It is affected only in its expression by your Incarnate Self. Sometimes there is a gulf between your Authentic Soul and your Incarnate Self consciousness.

The Battle Within

Do you know what the Gettysburg of your Spiritual Assiyah is? Have you ever experienced a time when there seemed to be an internal argument within yourself about what you think you **should** do and what you **want** to do? I call this the Gettysburg of the Incarnate Self. It is the civil war within. Where is this battleground exactly? How do you keep from being the war casualty?

Part of the process of gaining spiritual maturity is finding that you are being given more and more choices in Life. After you learn to outline your desire in detail to the Universe and God, and then say, "Either this or better" leaving the door open for the Holy One to help you choose, then you find that the Universe and God do not seem to be making a choice. It is left up to you to choose. This can be a painful time if you do not trust your intuition, your listening ability or your plain good sense. This can happen if you have been through some gut wrenching relationships that started out as if they were made in the stars and ended with you asking your Self what was that? Know that each relationship, each event, each experience was there by design (ludicrous as that may seem) for your higher enlightenment and elevation in the Light. It is like the time of a Saturn Return, when Papa Saturn is hemming you in at every turn until you have nowhere to turn, except within, this may be painful, but after you have crossed the precipice a new time to bloom dawns. (Maybe because of all the fertilizer you have been wading around in). So too, the time of Battle between your Authentic Soul and your Incarnate Self can be involved in this whole maturity process. It will mean your eventual freedom.

The battleground lies between your head and your heart in SA Assiyah, and sometimes your Authentic Soul. Your Spiritual Assiyah, your thoughts and emotions, are partly shaped by your experiences and partly shaped by your "hard wiring" that came with this chosen incarnation. It is all symbolic of your incarnation purposes and your Authentic Soul. Take for example the decision of becoming more deeply and emotionally involved with another person. Sometimes there is a civil war within you that pulls you in two directions or more. There are often conflicting emotions of love and fear. There are the thoughts of logic and experience. There is a sense of adventure and carefree joy and there can be a sense of anxiety and looming disaster! Your actions are frozen because your power plant, your emotions, are not fully engaged in your power of thought. How do you move forward in your actions and restore your sense of serenity and content-ment? How do you set your foot on your Path of Peace and stay with it? It helps if you center your consciousness in your Authentic Soul which is outside of time and space and which is not affected by the events in the physical world. As long as you base your consciousness in your Incarnate mind your thinking is subject to everything from what you have been eating and drinking to whether the sun is out or it has been raining buckets for days and you crave the boost of a sunny day. Your heart leads you in many ways, but it can also block your ability to think objectively and even transcend to hear the Still Small Voice of your Divine Guidance. The higher your emotions are running the more difficult it may be for you to hear. Learning the guided med-itation in the last chapter will help you transcend this block. In your Journal you will find an exercise for finding your Path of Peace. It will incorporate your knowledge of your Incarnate Self and the information you will receive from the meditations on Recovering Your Authentic Soul. In a changing world the process of finding your Path of Peace will enable you to make your decisions from a consciousness centered in your Authentic Soul, restoring your inner harmony. Harmony is not all the same vibration, it is vibrations that compliment each other. When you sing in harmony with another person you use one note that vibrates on one level and the other person sings on a different note, or level. Put them together and they compliment each other creating something more together than either is on its own. Harmony is the rainbow colors coming together to create a beautiful rainbow, something more wondrous than any color is on its own. Your Path of Peace will harmonize with the differing areas of your Life. You will feel at rest.

Both your AS and your SA/PA are always changing. Change is the nature of Being. Do you remember the three factors of the Worlds that we talked about in the last chapter? The physical world operates within the factors of time, space and Self. The Infinite worlds operate within the factors of mansions or fields, change and Soul. While your Incarnate Self is changing very quickly in time and space, your Authentic Soul is changing within the larger category of field or mansions toward The One Soul. It is the stabilizer that helps you stay on your intentions for your Self in this Dimension.

Harmony Between Your Authentic Soul and Incarnate Self

Part of the benefit of knowing the difference between your Authentic Soul and your Incarnate Self is being able to accept who you are in this incarnation. Knowing your Authentic Soul means you begin to see with awe and joy the Infinite Value of Being that you are as an emanation of The Source of Life. Then knowing the Incarnate Self you have chosen to be in this Lifetime enables you to embrace your Self whole-heartedly. This is Self-Acceptance. It is accepting the Self you are choosing to emanate as a ray of reflection from your Authentic Soul level. Self acceptance means accepting the shoe which fits and accepting that some shoes do not fit and that is okay. Trying to fit into and wear an ill-fitted shoe only hinders your pathway and indicates your non-acceptance of who you are. That indicates you are still centered in your finite Incarnate Self, embracing who you think you **should** be rather than who your Authentic Soul already enjoys being. You do not have to become your Authentic Soul, you already are! When you embrace your Authentic Soul you can then accept the gifts of your Incarnate Self. When you accept your Authentic Soul, in that knowledge that you have of it, you can accept the gifts it brings to you. Once you embrace it, you will begin receiving the joy and the gift of peace that it brings. Trust is also one of those gifts that is activated within you. The more you know of yourself the more you trust your Self. The more you live from that place of authenticity, the more you will also live with integrity. That is when others will begin to trust you.

You truly begin to live in trust of the evolution of the Light of the Universe and yourself, your Authentic Soul, as an intrinsic part of The Whole. You trust in the dynamic unfolding of God to be God, which includes the existence of you! You become aware that you are the shoes God created to walk around on Earth.

"Finding a pair of shoes that fit" means finding a place that **you** enjoy being and doing those things which **you** enjoy doing. Then you will find that your "shoes" support your feet in the pathway you desire to walk. The situations around you will support the pathway you desire to take. As you walk in joy and happiness you will attract positive people around you and open yourself to new opportunities for further joy. Your path of peace will also contribute to the larger good.

Your Authentic Soul is the Infinite and your Incarnate Self is the Finite. When you center on your Authentic Soul to motivate your Incarnate Self you are using the Infinite to affect the Finite, this World.

You also gain self acceptance as you begin to understand the principles of "choice". We are all given the gift of choice by the Creator. We have thousands of thoughts a day, but we are the ones who get to choose which thoughts we will hold and eventually act upon. Our choice is what empowers us. I have choice, and you have choice. When it comes to trying to get others to do what we want them to do what we are really asking them to do is to give up their God-given choice to us! Who are we to think we can take that choice from others? This is especially important in our closest relationships. When we honor our own empowerment of choice then we honor the choices of others all the more so.

Sometimes we look back in our lives and think "Oy! If I knew then what I know now I sure wouldn't have made that choice!" Well, guess what! If you didn't make that choice way back then, you wouldn't be who you are now. You know what you know now because you learned it by making that very choice back then! You are standing in more light now because of the choices you have made in your Life. So it doesn't serve you to judge yourself for your choices in the past, because they are your teachers. You made those choices standing in the light that you had at that time. Now you stand in more light, because of those choices.

You can bring your Incarnate Self into harmony with your Authentic Soul to gain financial freedom, personal safety and joy by being you. Centering on your Authentic Soul brings a deep contentment to your Life. How does centering on your Authentic Soul accomplish this in your Life?

Your Authentic Soul is debt free. The debts, including spiritual carry over such as karma that you now carry in your Incarnate Self, are malleable and changeable. While you are in this Lifetime you can change the energy you will carry out of this physical form back into spirit form, back to your Authentic Soul. Because your Authentic Soul is debt free when you bring your Incarnate Self into harmony with it you become debt free – one step at a time as you are given enlightenment from your Authentic Soul. When you ask for the wisdom to do this you open the portals that lets the Divine White Light flood through your Authentic Soul and into your Incarnate Self Spiritual Assiyah and finally through to Physical Assiyah through your wise and responsible actions. My advanced course on Financial Freedom gives you steps to follow to open to the flow of the Divine Plenty in your Life and to open your prosperity consciousness. Financial Freedom does not mean having so much money that you never fear lacking for anything again. That is bondage and servitude. Financial freedom means being free from the fear of lack. You could have a million dollars in your bank account and still be fearful that it will somehow disappear and you will not have enough. Stepping into the flow of the consciousness of your Source, and taking responsibility to open to the gates of ideas that you are given by inspiration, then falling in love with your ideas, birthing them in actions and nurturing them as you would a little child begins the process. You do not expect the child to feed you, but you nurture the child until it is old enough to be feeding you. Applying that principle to your work helps you to grow your prosperity and sustenance. You can use these principles in any area of your Life. You can even work on karma from this Lifetime and past Lifetimes. You can work on the purposes for your next Incarnation if you run out of debts from this Lifetime to pay off to others.

The first step to this freedom is to open your consciousness to the principle of freedom through choice. The choice is yours. You can choose in this moment your course of action and in the next moment and the next you will be given the option of choices again to refine your pathway. When you do not see options before you then you can ask your Angels to show you the options that are truly before you and expand your consciousness through angelic intervention, that you may make the choice which continues your Path of Peace. The first step to financial freedom is to realize that you are free. The freedom is not from lack, but from the fear of lack. Fear is always of the future. It has no energy because the future is not here yet. Therefore, to hold your fear you must use the energy of the moment of Now. This robs you of the energy you are given to live this moment of now. Instead you experience the low vibration of fear which freezes your actions.

Fear is the same vibrational energy wave as Love, except it is on the other end of the vibrational spectrum. It is a low vibration that creates a pull inward. You close up in fear. Love is a high vibrational energy that opens you up to others, to new ideas, to the world, to whatever you are facing. Love enables you to act in the face of fear which is true courage. When you stand in your Love you are able to bring yourself back to the moment of Now and truly live, every bodacious, succulent moment of Life. The power is yours for the power is in choice. The choice is yours: you can stand frozen in your fear, or move forward in your Love. They are the same emotion differing by degrees. That means if fear is present, so is Love. You have the choice. When you begin to think about your finances what is the predominant feeling? Where do you feel it? Is it fear or uneasiness? Do you feel it in the pit of your stomach, your chest, your throat? Where you are being affected in your body reveals how you think about money and finances. If you center your consciousness up in your Authentic Soul, the place beyond time and space, you are able to receive the inspired thoughts that come to fruition through your love and actions. In the advanced course Financial Freedom there are 10 Sacred Ways that are guidelines for putting your new consciousness of financial freedom as a choice into action.

When you are centering on your Authentic Soul, your Infinite Value, you become free of the condemnation and moral biases waged against you, even by your own mind about your performance, what you have, what you don't have. You know that you are of Infinite Value, no matter your financial profile or how many toys you possess or don't possess. You can then move to the process of shaping your financial future according to your desires. Your finances of this incarnation are changeable. They are what they are, but you are given choice each moment to do as you desire with them. You can ask for the help of grace in situations by Angelic intervention and you can ask for wisdom to know steps that will fill your treasure house. The Financial Freedom steps are Universal Principles such as reciprocity, cosmic ownership, and balanced exchanges that do not cause lack or create excesses, but promote prosperity. Just as centering your conscious thoughts in your Authentic Soul each day helps you to learn how to balance yourself in Financial Freedom – free from the fear of lack, opening your prosperity thinking and guiding you in wise choices it will also give you a sense of personal freedom to be yourself without fear of ostracizing thoughts, whether from others or your own. These are benefits of bringing your Incarnate Self into harmony with your Authentic Soul.

Your Authentic Soul is free of the "not good enough" messages you carry in your Incarnate Self. Some of these thoughts are from family background, peer pressure or cultural ills. They are about excess weight, "bad hair", no hair, too much hair, not smart enough, too smart, not sexy enough, too sexy or even "spiritual" inadequacies. Yes, even in our spiritual communities there come messages of what we "should" be – or not: you can't see auras, you don't hear from the Ascended Masters the way others seem to, you have difficulty "going somewhere" when you meditate alone, you don't feel healing energy in your hands or see visions of colors when you are doing your energy work? The list can go on and on. When we are centered upon our Authentic Soul we are free to ask for whatever gift of spirit we desire to use. But, the more you understand your Authentic Soul's purposes for this Incarnation the better you can understand your gifts of this Lifetime, including spiritual gifts.

As you explore your Authentic Soul you begin to remember past lives that somehow touch upon this Lifetime. You might learn that way back in Egypt you were a cracker-jack aura reader, but you can't see an aura in this Lifetime to save you. You can explore the "why" of the question and learn more about this Lifetime and thereby help you refine your path here and now. You may reopen that gift consciously; and in so doing learn how to consciously connect to that spiritual gift of aura reading. Or it may remain closed to you for purposes of focusing on other gifts. If you easily see everyone's aura it might more difficult for you to develop your sense of discernment from feeling their energy or weighing their words.

There is a scene in the movie *Ray* when he is a young boy who has just gone blind and he is asking his mother to help him. She stays quiet and out of his reach so he will learn that he can do what he thinks he cannot. In the movie, he was lying on the floor crying and he began to hear a cricket. He listened more intently and was able to eventually catch the cricket. The point is that sighted, his hearing would not have become so acute. How much of his music and rhythm came from the darken world of sight giving way to a higher sense of hearing? By the way, this movie also demonstrates the principles of the PA, body, reflecting what is happening in your SA, mind and emotions. Do you remember what event preceded Ray's eye disease? He saw his brother drown and did or could not save him! His eyes shut down to the world. He could not look at what he had done – or not done. He also turned to "narcotizing" himself later, seeking pleasurable feelings rather than the deep pain of his child's Soul, haunted by the events of his brother's death and his subsequent blindness. In all his success there was a nameless pain deep inside that did not go away. At the end of the movie his spiritual eyes are opened when he has a visitation from his deceased Mother, and he faces his pain in the light of her love. That experience had a profound effect on the rest of his Life. He found true strength and forgiveness for his own Self. Your Life here on Earth is connected with your Higher Eternal Being, your Authentic Soul. You are connected to your loved ones in the Higher Dimensions by the bridge of your love. You are supported and you have everything you need within you to live your incarnation. Your Authentic Soul can be a guide to you in your experiences and the use of your gifts. There are some people who are opening up in their Sacred Memory the gifts of previous Lifetimes, to heal this Lifetime in some way, or to use those gifts in service to others.

You can ask for the wisdom to know how to use or open to gifts you are seeking. We begin to open to what our gifts already are and how to further hone them for sacred work/play. In the Infinite Value of the Authentic Soul, we begin to really get it deep down inside, everything we need to deal with Life – this incarnation is there within us. We are Infinite Beings living a finite Lifetime. Our roots are within our infinite resources in our Authentic Soul. We can express whatever we embrace and give ourselves over to the sheer joy and ecstasy of truly loving what we do.

It means waking up in the morning and thinking, "I love being me!" This is personal security. You are secure in being and expressing you, because whether other people embrace it or even understand it or not does not touch on your Infinite Value. You are you, you are Infinite in your Eternal Value in your Being, your existence. As you live and express your highest aspiration you vibrate at a higher and higher level, attracting those of the higher vibrations that are in harmony to you and opening new opportunities for yourself. **The more you live what you love, the more you will love what you live.**

You live a Life of joy and contentment. Your joy is the overflow of love from your heart as you open yourself and share yourself with the world. In so expressing this deep level of your Being in joy every day your Authentic Soul is at rest. It is flowing through your Incarnate Self into the World of Doing. You feel fulfillment of your Being. All of this translates to contentment. There is a deep quiet in your Soul. In joy you are content.

You can live from your integrity unapologetically. You decorate your body, your home, your environment, you choose activities creatively, you move away from all the shoulds. You make choices standing in your love, living more consciously and purposefully, every juicy moment! You awaken in the morning able to say, "I love being Me!" You do this one day after the other, like the layers of an onion, going deeper as you transverse the layers of your own Being.

The actions you choose can bring you into harmony with your

Authentic Soul or not. You can stand in your love or in your fear. You can refine your Soul, you can shine brighter, and love stronger. It is your choice. You are God's Love made manifest in this physical world. You are Infinite. You are Eternal. You are. How do you say that for your Self? **I AM.**

As you begin to think, feel and act authentically you experience
- Inspired creative thoughts (coming from Above) regardless of your situation
- Overflow of Love from your heart (coming from Above) beyond experience
- Body glows with Higher Level vibrations (you are just glowing today!)
- **Truth**: As I center my consciousness on my Authentic Soul I change physically, for my physical being is a manifestation, a mirroring of the Higher Levels of my Being.
- You begin to emanate your Authentic Soul into the world around you

Living from your integrity you unapologetically
- decorate your body accordingly
- decorate your home and environment
- choose your activities from your creativity
- move away from actions of "shoulds"
- make choices of actions standing in your Love
- live more and more consciously, fully living every juicy moment
- awaken in the morning thinking and feeling "I love being me. It is so much fun!"

You Experience Being Free!

Journal Pages

"Lech Lecha" "Go to Your Self"

The Divine Voice said, **"Lech Lecha"** "Go to yourself". When you go to your Authentic Soul you follow the trail leading you back to The Source, as well, your beginning and your destiny.

The following exercise will help you explore your Incarnate Self as you know it. It will lead you on your bread crumb trail back to your Authentic Soul. Knowing these unique aspects of your Being will help you when you are making decisions in your Life to stay true to your Authentic Soul, to live your integrity.

Know Your Preferences:

1. Make a list of your likes, what are your favorites?

Climate:

Terrain and Water:

Environment:

Cultures:

Animals:

Birds:

Fish:

Architecture:

Structural Materials:

Furniture:

Foods:

Interior Design themes:

Clothing:

Colors:

Time of Day:

Seasons:

Holidays:

Rituals:

Divine Beings: (Angels and Archangels, Ascended Masters, Spirit Guides, Animal Guides, Faeries, Sprites, Elves, Tree People, Leprechauns, Dwarves, etc., etc.,)

2. How have these changed over the years? Do you still like the same things? Put a check by the things you listed above which are still things you like.

3. How have you spiritually changed over the years?

4. What is the correlation between how your preferences have changed over the years and how you have spiritually changed over the years?

5. Put a star * next to the likes that you listed which you remember first liking in your childhood.

6. Briefly describe three of the happiest and most fulfilling events of your Life (Childhood or adult). Which elements that you listed as your likes were present or part of those events?

You are vibrating at a particular rate. Everything in existence carries its own vibrational energy and rate. When you encounter that which is vibrating at a rate harmonious to yours it is a pleasant sensation, an easy fit. Your **dislikes** are those things which are **not** in harmony with your own vibration. They do not resonate with you. Your body, emotions and mental vibrations will try to come into sync with those around you. This can lead to feelings of chaos and disharmony within you. When you learn what things are in harmony with you then you can surround yourself with that which heightens your vibrations and let go of that which does not resonate with you without guilt. You can make adjustments to those situations which you do not have a choice in, such as the color of the room in which you work at the corporate offices of your international corporation employer. You will learn how and what you can add to your private space that will restore harmony for you without needing to adjust the world to you. This is learning the balance of adjusting to the world, as well as adjusting your world to you.

As your consciousness grows and widens so does your awareness of and relationship to these categories. Enlightenment brings illumination into the Divine in all of Creation. In this illumination of your Incarnate Self through harmony with your Authentic Soul you begin to truly live Life, enjoying every juicy moment of it!

Purposes of Your Incarnation

The Faerie Tales, childhood stories, and Biblical tales that you liked best often reveal the themes and purposes of your present Incarnation. As you look back on those favored stories see if you can pick up a theme that runs through all of them, weaving together the cloth from which this incarnation is cut.

1. List three stories or Faerie Tales you liked best as a child.

    a.

    b.

    c.

2. Retell each story in your mind, or find a copy of the story and reread it.

3. Write a sentence about each story's main theme.

    a.

    b.

    c.

4. What did you like best in each story?

    a.

    b.

    c.

5. What part did you dislike most in each story?

    a.

    b.

    c.

6. What did you fear the most in each story?

    a.

    b.

    c.

7. Who was your hero or heroine when you were a child? Who did you want to be like? (This modeling can be who you most often chose to "act out" when you were playing "let's pretend" games. It can be a person, an animal, Faeries, Angels or anyone you liked to pretend you were. Who were your favorite comic book or story book characters? These will give you insight as to who your Soul relates to!)

8. What were the characteristics of that person, animal or Being?

9. What gift did they bring to the World?

10. What gift did they bring to others?

11. What supernatural power/s did they have?

12. In what way have you called forth these gifts and powers in your Life?

13. Look at all the answers you have filled in about your stories and your model. Below, write what themes begin to appear over and over through them.

14. How have these stories foretold your Incarnation Purposes and Themes? How do they paint of portrait of your Incarnate Self?

Your Incarnate Self can be influenced by your Authentic Soul if you so choose. However, in your SA, there can be a battleground of civil war (Gettysburg) within you. You may experience a tug-of-war between your desire and your fears. The back and forth of your thoughts and feelings keep you from moving forward in your actions. How can you bring a truce to these bloodied fields?

Here are some questions (dialogue) you can ask your Self and steps that you can take to lead you to your Path of Peace and render unto you the harmony that you seek.

1. **Notice when you are in a mental and emotional battle.** Being aware that you are going back and forth and not taking action is the first step to finding Peace.

2. **What is your desire?** List what it is that you want. This is an important question. Take some time to think about it, for sometimes when we weigh the pros and cons of a decision and try to figure out the means by which we will manifest our desire we lose sight of the true desire itself. For instance, an elderly woman may wish that she had a daughter. When the deeper desire is explored it may be that she wants someone to take care of her the way she took care of her elderly parents. The daughter was the solution her mind jumped to without consciously identifying the true desire.

The conflict usually comes in confusing the pathway to the desire, or solution to obtaining the desire with the desire itself. The value is usually within the pathway itself, for the process often carries as much treasure in it as the end result, or desire.

Your Desire:

Pathway A to your Desire:

Pathway B to your Desire:

3. What is in harmony with your Authentic Soul? There is rarely only one path to your Desire. By exploring your options, or opening your mind to hear from your Angelic or Divine Guidance or your Authentic Soul for options (pathways) you have not thought of, you more clearly define **Your Desire**. You can do this by doing the "Path of Peace" test.

- Think about each path you are deciding between.
- Imagine yourself taking each path to your desire one at a time.
- Do you feel peace on this pathway or that one? A or B?
- Do you feel unrest with one of the pathways?
- If you are at peace with a pathway it is in harmony with your Authentic Soul.
- If you are at unrest in any way, your Authentic Soul is still sending you messages to help you adjust the pathway for harmony.

4. Where is your Path of Peace?

5. What do you choose to *do*?

In the next chapter on **Meditations**, you will be transcending up to the Higher Realms through the Four Worlds. In the Highest Realm visited in the Crystal Palace Meditation, you will be recording the contents of the rooms you visit there in your Journal Pages. To continue the Path of Peace test you can take Your Desire into each room and look at it in the Light of that room for this incarnation. After you have gone into the four rooms with your desire you will have much more information on where the Path of Peace is for you.

Notes

Chapter Four

Meditations

Introduction

Now that you have the background of the last three chapters and have worked in your journal we are going to venture together into the Meditative Journeys that will help you explore deeper or higher parts of your Authentic Soul. We are going to move through your Incarnate Self Physical Assiyah, Spiritual Assiyah and then up to Yetzirah, and the Crystal Palace of B'riyah. There you will enter four rooms to meet different aspects of your Authentic Soul. After that you will ascend the Grand Staircase to approach Atzilut and the consciousness that touches upon the unimaginable. The meditation will not lead you into Atzilut because to cross the chasm means to dissolve the Differentiated you, and there would not be a "you" to return from that place. You will descend in safety and wholeness back down the Grand Staircase and you will begin opening to the consciousness of Your Authentic Soul.

You are going to start with a grounding meditation that you can use each time you are taking a meditative journey to the Higher Dimensions. It is important to ground your Energy because you are going to be opening to the high vibrational energy of the Higher Dimensions. This works exactly like a lightning rod. If a bolt of lightning strikes an ungrounded barn it burns the barn, damages the structure or even blows it apart. However, if you attach a metal rod to the barn and run it down the side and into the ground, the lightning will follow the path of the metal rod down into Mother Earth, who can handle that amount of energy. When you are meditating and opening yourself to very high energy (even in healing practices) it is important to ground your body, opening the portals above you and below you so Mother Earth can receive the energy. In that way you are not running the high energy through your cellular body. If you have ever felt light headed or slightly queasy in your stomach while meditating or doing intense healing modalities that is an indication that you need to stop and re-ground yourself, for your body is responding to the energy overload. Drinking a lot of water is also recommended because that "rinses" you cells, and acts as not only a washing but a cooling system. The grounding exercise at the beginning of the meditation can be used anytime you begin any meditation.

After each meditation, record your experiences that you are able to remember from the meditation. You will use information from the meditations in your Journal Pages and then use those pieces of information to further experience a new consciousness of your Incarnate Self and your Authentic Soul. Please see the back of the book for obtaining these meditations on CD.

Meditative Journeys Overview

Assiyah
Physical Assiyah – **Your Elemental Body Meditation**
Spiritual Assiyah
    SA Yetzirah – **All You Feel at Once Meditation**
    SA B'riyah – **Power of Envisioning Meditation**
Yetzirah – Rainbow of Yetzirah Meditation
B'riyah – Crystal Palace of B'riyah Meditation

Atzilut – Grand Staircase Meditation

Elemental Body Meditation
Physical Assiyah

Become comfortable, the way you always sit or lie for meditation.

Take in three deep breaths (spirit), breathing out fully each time and refilling fully with each breath.

Focus on a space about six inches above your head. This is the Crown, Keter.

It is a sphere, round and flexible. Allow it to open and dilate.

Let the crystalline Divine White Light from above flood into your Being through that opening.

Breathe it in and draw it down into your head, completely filling your head, through your ears and deeply flowing down through your neck.

As you breathe let it flow down in to your chest cavity and let it fill your chest with Light.

Now breathe the warm White Light down into your left arm all the way to your hand and your fingers. Breathe it down into your right arm, hand and fingers.

Let the White Light flow into your abdomen, filling it and clearing it, putting all your organs into Divine Order and adjusting your body into harmony.

Feel the White Light flow down into your place of reproduction, filling your organs with creative Energy.

Now let the Divine Light flow down your left leg, through to your foot and out the sole of your foot into the ground. When you are finished let the Divine Light flow down your right leg through your knee, down to your foot and out the sole of your foot, forming roots that grow down into the ground.

Now let the roots carry the Divine White Light deeper and deeper, wider and wider down into the Earth, deeper through the layers of the Earth's crust, deeper and wider, until the roots go into the core of Mother Earth.

Mother Earth supplies the elements from which the body has risen. Feel the White Hot, yet different, heavier, denser Energy of Mother Earth.

Let the Energy of the core of Mother Earth begin to travel up the roots of Energy all the way to the soles of your feet, up your legs, through the knees, up through your thighs, your reproductive organs, your abdomen, filling your abdomen and coming together with the Crystalline Energy of the Divine Light White from above centering in your Heart. It may feel like a little shock as these two Energies mesh.

Now you are quite grounded and yet flowing with a High Level of Divine White Energy.

In this space, thank your elemental body for being the vessel of Light that it is for you.

Thank each part of your body for what it does for you. Thank your head, your neck, your arms, hands and fingers, your chest, your abdomen and all of its organs, thank your reproductive organs, the seed of potential within you, your legs, your feet and your toes.

Pause

Choose the area of your body that you like the least and ask that body part what it does for you.

Pause

As you begin to understand that body part, say "thank you" to it for what it does for you. Appreciate what it does. Speak your words of peace to it. Speak your words of assurance and love to it.

Pause

Now feel the elements of Mother Earth in your body. First allow yourself to be in consciousness of the part of you that is Earth, the sinews, the ligaments, the tendons, muscles and bones, fascia, the connective tissue, the skin, the cells. All of this manifests the rich Earth and connects you to the World of Action, the World of Assiyah.

Pause

And now move to the element of water. Feel the water within your being. Feel the fluids that are in your blood moving the cells of your blood around your body. Feel the fluids in your digestive tract. Feel the fluids carrying the poisons out of your body in your sweat and in your urine. Feel the fluids that surround your brain acting as a pillow so it can float weightlessly. Feel the moisture of the water in your mouth, your saliva. Feel the fluids that carry the seeds and eggs of Life. These fluids symbolize and connect you to the World of Emotion, the World of Yetzirah in the water of your body. Thank it for all it does for you.

Pause

Now move to the element of air within your body and bloodstream, carrying oxygen to all parts of your body. Become aware of the air in your lungs, and the air moving up and down through your throat and through your nose. Notice the air that flows through your vocal cords that you may create with your speech. The element of air connects you with the World of Thought, the World of B'riyah. This breath connects you with the next symbol of element, which is Spirit, the fire within your body.

Pause

Become conscious of the electrical, the fire within your body, the electrical charges in your brain, the electrical charges going down your spine, out your nerves to all parts of your body, sensitizing and awakening a consciousness within you. Become aware of the electrical sparks jumping between your cells, the synapses of your cells, connecting, opening consciousness, and traversing moving energy. Feel the energy moving through your electrical circuitry; it is fire, representing Spirit. It is the inspiriting, the inhabiting, and the integration of your body with your Spirit.

Pause

Now feeling awake and alive and tingling in all your parts, set an intention to most fully experience and express your Authentic Soul through your Incarnate Self. Open your consciousness to this incarnation's purposes as you live your Life.

Pause

When you are ready, take deep breaths and with each breath return your consciousness to this time and this place. As you do so allow Keter to remain open to the flow, but closed enough so you can become present and conscious to this room and those who are around you.

When you are ready open your eyes. Stretch out your arms so you can fully inhabit your body. Stretch out your legs.

All You Feel At Once Meditation
SA Yetzirah

Become comfortable, the way you always sit or lie for meditation.
Take in three deep breaths (spirit), breathing out fully each time and refill. Follow the grounding meditation at the beginning of the Body Meditation. When you have set your grounding, begin below:

Become aware of the area of your heart.

See your heart begin to open in the safety of your own Presence.

What do you feel at this moment? (Remember, Peace is not an emotion, but a state of Being)

What emotion do you feel; joy, happiness, love, anger, fear?

Feel it, and truly allow yourself to experience that feeling.

Where else do you feel a sensation in your body?

Your emotions also affect your elemental body. How is the emotion you are feeling affecting your elemental body right now?

What thought is attached to this emotion?

Let go of that emotion, and watch it return to your heart.

Open your heart and allow another feeling to emerge.

What is this feeling you have? Truly let yourself experience how it feels.

Name that feeling. Where else in your body do you have a sensation connected to that feeling? What thought arises as you feel this emotion?

Are these two feelings quite different? Do they feel different? Yet they are both within you at the same time.

Centering again on your chest area, what are other feelings you have experienced in your heart this week?

Out of all these feelings, which do you desire to have as the dominant feeling within you every day? What is the base feeling you desire to have in your heart every day? Name that information as your baseline or foundational emotion. Set your intention to re-center yourself on this feeling whenever you lose touch with it in your consciousness. It is a major Energy flow from your Authentic Soul which empowers your actions.

Thank each and every emotion you are able to feel, from Life-freezing fear to great joy and overflowing love for the power they provide for you. Thank each of your emotions.

Thank your heart for holding the power and energy and the multiplicity of emotions which serve you.

These emotions lead you to your Spiritual B'riyah, your World of Thought.

Take deep breaths and with each breath return your consciousness to this time and this place. Softly and gently awaken to this room. When you are ready, become present to this room and all that is around you.

Power of Envisioning
SA B'riyah

Become comfortable, the way you always sit or lie for meditation.
Take in three deep breaths (spirit), breathing out fully each time and refill. Ground your meditation in the same way you did on the first meditation. Then begin with the meditation below:

Relax your body to the chair, drop your shoulders, release all the tension in your body.

Move your attention up into the center of your head, between your ears, in the very center of your head.

Visualize a doorway. It is the doorway to your mind.

Approach the door, open it and move through it into a place where

there are pictures, which is the first language of the brain.
Picture a baby lying in a crib. You are that baby.
You are a newborn looking up from your crib at your world.

You see someone lean over the crib, smiling at you and picking you up with gentle care, holding you securely.

You recognize this face and this person as one who always holds you close, warms you with their body and gives you sweet substance that fills and satisfies you.

There is recognition and feeling, but no name. This is vision – without spoken language. It is the first language of B'riyah, the power of intellect, of thought. This carries the power to connect the vision of this person with the feeling of loving gentleness.

Now this loving person has put you back into the crib. You are alone.

You desire to have this person near to you and to feel them comfort you.

You envision their image as you experience the feelings you desire. This loving person is not there, but remember what they look like and you see a vision of them before your mind's eye.

This is your first envisioning. You are seeing the vision on the in-side.

You cry out to the envisioned person and this person appears before your crib.

You have manifested their presence by your summons. You have called them forth by your envisioning of them and your actions, the vibrations of your voice which are empowered by your feelings.

Your thought in a picture or vision, connected to feelings and expressed through a voice, has become manifest in the physical world around you. In time your pictures will be expressed in more detailed and precise words. You have learned the power to call unto you physical substance from your vision.

Thank your mind for giving you the pictures from within.

Note who this loving person is in your Life.

Thank their Authentic Soul for their care of you.

What powers of vision do you seek to gain? Set your intention for your Incarnate Self to see with your inner vision from the truth and integrity of your Authentic Soul.

Open to your Authentic Soul that it may flow down to you, to your Incarnate Self's envisioning mind, the visions of your future.

When you do this you will move your conscious from the World of Assiyah, doing, action, the physical world, to the Infinite Worlds beyond your Incarnation Self.

When you are ready, take deep breaths and with each breath return your consciousness to this time and this place. When you are ready gently open your eyes, and become present to this room and those around you.

Introduction To The
Meditations On The Higher Realms

You are tapping into Infinite Yetzirah, Infinite B'riyah and Atzilut. These are the realms from which your Authentic Soul is sourced and emanated. Exploring these Higher Dimensions requires an opening of consciousness within to a place that is "no place" beyond. You will follow your own Incarnate Self up into the Higher Realms to experience your Authentic Soul.

Placed within you is Eternal Life. This Eternal Life is the action of breathing in the World of Assiyah. As you enter this finite world your first action is to breathe in, Yod-hey and the last action as you leave this world is to breathe out, Vav-hey. Thus your Life is a series of breaths, each giving your elemental body oxygen, the power name of God, Yod-Hey, Vav-Hey, Yod-Hey, Vav-Hey. Each breath also gives your SA inspiration, the bringing in of spirit. It creates a keyway, an opening of the Dimensions through which the Energy of your Being can ascend in consciousness to the Higher Dimensions, to the Source and to the dwelling place of your Authentic Soul.

You experience your Authentic Soul when you access it in this meditation place through the keyway and you manifest it in SA and PA, through your thoughts, feelings, actions and physical body. In this way you open your Incarnate Self's consciousness to your Authentic Soul consciousness. You then experience living in harmony and contentment throughout your fully human experience. This is a balance, not a static state. When you learned to walk it was not just a matter of learning to put one foot in front of the other and shifting your weight, it also incorporated being able to navigate according to changing surfaces of footing. You walk differently across rocky terrain than you do a smooth sidewalk. You shift your weight differently when you walk up a steep incline than you do when you are navigating down a steep hill. So too, harmony within your SA and PA shifts according to events in your Life, and shifts of balance are necessary to find your harmony between your Incarnate Self and your Authentic Soul is an ever changing balance. **Living and experiencing your Authentic Soul is an ever-changing balance of truly being at home in your Incarnated Body.**

Rainbow of Infinite Yetzirah

In the following meditations for Infinite Yetzirah and Infinite B'riyah you will be taken outside of time and space. However, in order to do this within your Incarnate Self you will be guided to use symbolic representations such as the Rainbow and the Crystal Palace. Those places do not exist in physical form in the Higher Dimensions, but in Energy and in Spirit form. This symbolism helps you focus your Energy and create a *chasmal*, as it is called in Hebrew. Chasmal is like a blue electric field to give Energy form to carry our consciousness to the place beyond "place". You will experience these meditations in whatever way you experience them. Your visions will be meaningful to you. There is no right or wrong way to experience them.

You will move from the Rainbow of Infinite Yetzirah directly into the Crystal Palace of Infinite B'riyah. These two meditations are created to follow one another as one meditation.

Face the West for this meditation, for the West is the direction of New Beginnings. We draw upon the power of the West for New Beginnings. You are beginning a new phase of your spiritual journey.

Become comfortable, the way you always sit for meditation.

Take in three deep breaths (spirit), breathing out fully each time and refilling yourself fully with each breath. Start with your grounding meditation, and when you are ready begin:

From the place of SA B'riyah, visions, envision a beautiful white fluffy cloud.

Walk into that cloud.

We allow that cloud to take us outside of time and space on our journey. Feel its cool moisture on your face, and the cloud's softness beneath your feet.

Let it envelop you until it is before you, behind you, beneath you and above you, until you no longer know which direction you are facing.

Behind you a Light is shining and illumining the Cloud.

It is forming a beautiful radiant rainbow before you.

Walk up to the shining multicolored water droplets and touch them.

You walk **into** each of the colors of the rainbow individually. You walk into the red color.

You are standing with the red of the rainbow all around you. Breathe it in. Experience the red.

What are you feeling as you experience the redness of the Rainbow?

Pause

Now you walk into orange droplets. They are all around you. What are you feeling in this place of orange? Breathe it in.

Pause

Now you walk into the yellow color of the rainbow. All around you is yellow. What do you feel here in yellow? Breathe it in.

Pause

Now you step into the portion of the rainbow that is green. Every drop of cloud is green. What is the feeling of this green? Breathe it in. Feel it.

Pause

Now as you leave green you walk into the blue place in the rainbow. How do you feel in this blue place? Breathe it in.

Finally you step into the violet droplets of the radiant rainbow. You see violet all around you. What feeling does the Energy of violet call forth from within you? Breathe it in.

Pause

You have walked out of the rainbow now. Carry the radiance of each color still vibrating with feeling within your heart. The feelings in your heart are as pure as the colors of the radiant rainbow.

Begin to walk out of the cloud now into the deep blue expanse of the sky.

Move from the water of the cloud of Yetzirah, emotion, to the clear air of B'riyah, the power of intellect.

The Crystal Palace of B'riyah

Breathe in deeply. The air is different, crisp, soft, clear, and crystalline.

You vibrate at a Higher Level with each breath.

You begin to feel very light and you see more clearly, more vividly than ever before.

You see a palace a short distance away. It is gleaming and radiant with Light. It is your mansion, your palace, a place of clarity for you.

You walk up the pathway to the palace gates. As you step on the threshold the doors open wide for you.

Once inside you see a grand entry way. The chandelier above you glows, illumining the entire palace with Divine White Light.

There are many doorways around you and a Grand Staircase before you.

You know you will go up the staircase, but not until you have explored the doorways and rooms of this floor.

Walk over to the doorway on your left. Open the door and walk in.

It is a room filled with relationships. The Divine White Light from the Chandelier is illuminating the Divine Light in each Soul in the room.

You watch as one Soul steps forward toward you.

In the Divine Light of the Great Chandelier you see that Soul's Divine Light. How does that Soul look to you? What symbols is it using to represent its relationship to others?

As you walk up to that Soul notice the Divine Light enfolding both your Light and their Light. Be there with that Soul in the Light. Stay there as long as you like.

Now move away from that Soul. What thought comes to your consciousness?

What feeling is attached to that thought?

Hold the vision, the thought and this feeling sacred in your heart as you slowly back away and leave this room.

This is a vision of your Authentic Soul as it is in relationship to others. Put this vision in your Sacred Heart, for this is you. You never have to vary from this Soul. This Soul is you – a symbolic vision of your Authentic Soul as it moves out to relate to others.
As you re-enter the entry-way you move to the next doorway on the left.

As you open the door the room is filled with Light and you see it is a room of vocations, the calling of the Soul. These are pathways to Sacred Service in God, the Divine Light.

You see a pathway which calls to you by becoming brighter and brighter in the Chandelier's illumining Light.

You place your right foot upon the pathway. What is happening?

Everything around you has changed. How has it changed?

Stand on your pathway, walk on your pathway, and be in your pathway.

As you walk, where is your pathway leading you? How is it leading you? What is this pathway?

Your pathway is always available for you to re-enter and gain a vision for direction.

What inspired thoughts do you receive on your pathway?

What do you intend to do with those thoughts? Set an intention to recall those thoughts and to put them into action.

What do you feel when you are on your pathway? Place these inspired visions in your Sacred Heart and begin to back towards the door.

Go through the door and back into the great entry-way and into the brilliant Light from the Great Chandelier.

This vision is a symbolic representation of your Authentic Soul. It is the Pathway of You, at this time in your life.

On the opposite side of the entry-way is another door. Move toward that door.

As you approach it the door springs open and you find yourself instantly inside. The Light from the Great Chandelier illumines this room. It is a Ballroom, a place that is dancing and vibrating with the rhythms of Life. It is shimmering with Light and vibrational Energy.

Walk toward the center of the room. Notice the colors, the patterns of the floor, the ceiling and the walls.

On the walls all around you are golden mirrors. Each mirror reflects the face of a Soul. Each reflected Soul wears a different garb and each one emits colored Lights.

One looks directly at you. Walk over to that image in the mirror. What is that Soul wearing? What colors surround them?

Place your hands palm to palm with theirs and look directly into their eyes and move through the pupil of their eye, the window of their Soul.

There you experience the Light radiating and glistening.

Come into harmony with that radiation, the rhythm, the movement of that Light. Breathe it in. Come up to its level until you are radiating, glistening and moving in Light with it. How does this level of vibration feel?

Be there.

Allow a word to form before you. What word forms in the midst of the radiating Light?

Look into the word until you enter the word.

Now bring the entire word and its vibrational energy into your Sacred Heart.

This is the essential word of your Authentic Soul. This word describes your essence, and your Being; who you are authentically.

Place this word as a seal upon your Sacred Heart. It is a guiding Light, a beacon emanating from your Authentic Soul. As you speak this word it will always lead you home again.

Breathe this word in. Stay with it as long as you like.

Then begin to back out of the mirror, and the Ballroom, the place of the vibrational energy of the rhythms of Life.

As you back through the doorway into the great entry-way you see a door at the foot of the Grand Staircase.

It is the last door before you ascend the Stairs.

It is the last room of the differentiations that make up your Authentic Soul. How does this door look?

Place your hand on the doorknob. Turn it, opening the door wide. What is it like to open this door?

The room is dark. Invite the Light from the Great Chandelier to enter and the room through you, to illumine this room of mystery.

The Light comes into your hand and a ray of Light emits from the palm of your hand to illumine the room.

Walk around the room and lift your hand to illumine the contents, the walls, the decorations. This mystery room is filled with treasures.

One area calls you over to explore it in the Light. It has been eternally cloaked in the mystery of Sacred Darkness. You illumine this treasure in the Divine Light for the first time.

You stare at it in wonder. As you sit down it begins to reveal itself to you in the Divine Light of your hand.

You hear it speak to you. I am you. I am in you and you in me. I am part of Your Being in the Universe. You help create the Universe by being You, Me.

Just be and hear its Voice. Ask it your questions. Hold its answers in your Sacred Heart.

This is the treasure of the Authentic You. You are experiencing the special treasure which is your Authentic Soul's heart.

Aztilut

Follow this treasure, the heart of your Authentic Soul up the Grand Staircase. Let this treasure lead you.

As you ascend the Staircase the Divine Light from the Great Chandelier shines brighter and brighter until you can no longer see the stairs below your feet. You can no longer feel them.

The Bright Light envelops you.

It begins to sparkle.

The illumined sparkles begin to move apart, dissipating.

All of your Being is dissipating with them until there is no form or shape or color.

The sparkles become fainter and fainter in the dispersed Light until there is Nothing.

There is no breath.

Pause

Take a deep breath. With this breath you bring back into consciousness your differentiated Authentic Soul, your individuality made of The Light. You bring your Soul back from the brink of Nothingness in this breath.

You can now experience Being, your Authentic Soul. You are once again a living, breathing, conscious part of Creation. Without you, Creation is not whole.

You are shining from your Being. Radiate and feel the Divine Light that is You.

Look back over the symbols within each room.

Your Divine and Infinite Authentic Soul is symbolized in the Treasure from the Mystery Room.

You are the Word from the mirrored image in the Ballroom.

You are the Pathway in the room of Divine Invocation.

You are the glowing Divine Soul in the room of Relationships.

Your Crystalline Palace is your dwelling place of authenticity. Your Soul is at home here. The rhythmic heartbeat of this palace is your own Eternal heartbeat.

Breathe deeply and begin to walk away from the Palace. With every breath you renew your Authentic Soul, your differentiation in and of the Light.

Walk from the Crystal Palace and that airy blue place of B'riyah into the dewy moist Rainbow Clouds of Yetzirah.

Embrace the glow of your emotions, your feelings which put you in touch with the world of differentiation around you.

Now, with a deep breath move back into your elemental body.

Fully bring the inspirational thoughts from the Blue Place of the B'riyah Palace into your Assiyah mind and memory.

Securely lodge the feelings of the Rainbow Cloud of Yetzirah into your Assiyah, Sacred Heart.

Stand up gently with your eyes still closed.

Breathe deeply again bringing the consciousness of your Authentic Soul down into your elemental body. Bring it down from your head, through your neck and stretch out your arms to let it fill them, down through your chest, down your abdomen, and down to your legs. Shake each leg as you fill it with your Authentic Soul's Divine Light, down to your feet and toes and across the soles of your feet.

Now stand on Mother Earth and let your Authentic Soul blend with and unite with the Divine Elements of this planet through your incarnated Being.

Bring the Light of your Authentic Soul back up to the area of your heart and seat your Authentic Soul in your Incarnate Self there.

When you are ready, return to this room, open your eyes and become Present.

You have recovered the consciousness of your Authentic Soul. You can return to this consciousness every day, or whenever you want to.

You are God's Love made manifest in physical form. You are an emanation of God. Now you can answer the question:

Created in the image of God, who does that mean I am?

God's A.S._____.

Write your name in the blank space and read what it says out loud. God's Authentic Soul – <u>your name</u>. Just think who that means you are! You are intrinsic to God. You are not the totally of Being, but are essential to Being.

In Love, You Are.

Please say that out loud right now, for your Self:

"I AM"

Chapter Five

Meditations

Keys to your Authentic Soul

Elemental Body Meditation
Physical Assiyah

 How did your body feel when you came back from this meditation?

 Where did you identify the "four elements" in your body?

Earth

Water

Air

Fire

 What part did you choose as your least favorite part of your body?

What did it say it does for you?

Did you make peace with it as you connected to it in love and thanked it for what it does?

How does your relationship with your body differ now than before this meditation?

All You Feel At Once
Spiritual Assiyah
Yetzirah

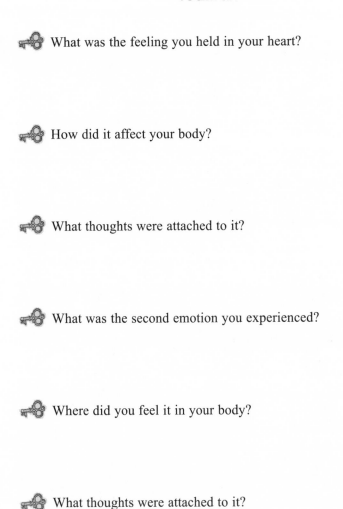

What was the feeling you held in your heart?

How did it affect your body?

What thoughts were attached to it?

What was the second emotion you experienced?

Where did you feel it in your body?

What thoughts were attached to it?

The Power of Envisioning
Spiritual Assiyah
B'riyah

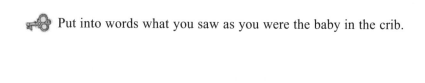

Put into words what you saw as you were the baby in the crib.

Who came to hold you?

How did you get that person to come back to you?

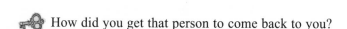

How does that relate to the way you communicate your needs to others now?

When you want to envision something you can go to this process of envisioning and calling from your Authentic Soul the pre language vision. Have a relationship with that vision through your emotions. Then summon that vision into this Dimension through the words of your mouth. What would you like to envision and manifest at this time in your Life?

Date when you experience the manifestation in your Life of the vision you wrote about in the question above. How did it look? How different did it look in the physical world once it was manifest?

The Rainbow of
Infinite Yetzirah

How did the cloud feel to you?

How did it feel to be enveloped by the cloud?

How did the redness feel to you?

How did the orange place feel?

How did the yellow place feel?

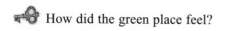 How did the green place feel?

How did the blue place feel?

How did the violet place feel?

What was your favorite place? Why?

How did you feel as you left the rainbow cloud for the clear blue air?

The Crystal Palace of Infinite B'riyah

Describe how your Crystal Palace looked.

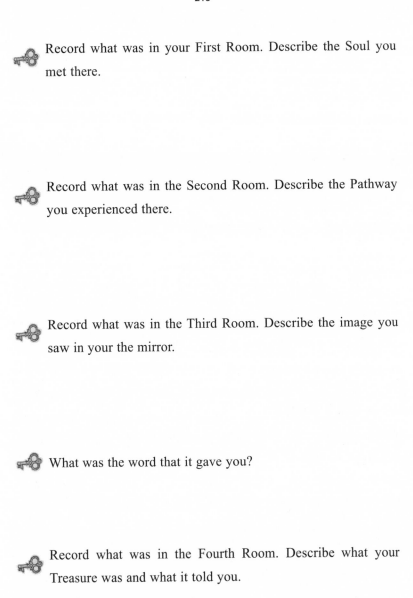

Record what was in your First Room. Describe the Soul you met there.

Record what was in the Second Room. Describe the Pathway you experienced there.

Record what was in the Third Room. Describe the image you saw in your the mirror.

What was the word that it gave you?

Record what was in the Fourth Room. Describe what your Treasure was and what it told you.

Using your Keys to Unlock the Symbols of Your Meditation

Room One

 Relations – The symbols of your first room show you how you relate from your Authentic Soul to others.

What are the characteristics of the Soul you saw?

Example:

I saw a huge, plump, white Mother Rabbit. Her heart was large and she was very soft and welcoming to me. When I was a child I ate from "Bunnikins" dishes from Royal Doulton china which had illustrations from the Tales of Peter Rabbit on them. The Peter Rabbit stories were my favorite childhood stories. I had forgotten about those dishes until this meditation. I asked myself, what are the characteristics of Rabbit? What did her heart symbolize? What did her plump and welcoming appearance symbolize – how do I relate to those descriptions? What part did Mother Rabbit play in the Peter Rabbit stories? These are symbolic representations of my Authentic Soul as it relates to others in this Lifetime.

Now you can take the description of the Soul you saw in your first room and interpret the symbols as you connect their meaning to you, personally. Do this with each of the images you saw in all four rooms.

Room Two

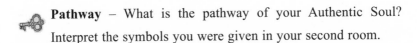 **Pathway** – What is the pathway of your Authentic Soul? Interpret the symbols you were given in your second room.

Room Three

Essence – What word is the essence of your Authentic Soul? Interpret the symbols and word you received in your third room.

Room Four

Treasure – From the symbols of this room what is the nature of the mystery unfolding as the Heart's Treasure of Your Authentic Soul for this Lifetime?

Example:

I saw a Lion who spoke words of Presence to me. In my natal chart, the Zodiac sign that my Saturn is in is Leo, (the Lion) in my 8th House. The characteristics of a Lion, the Planet Saturn energy, the personality effects of the Zodiac sign Leo and the 8th House are all things I explored to understand the meaning of this vision. Leo the Lion is the ruler of the 5th House, so everything connected with 5th House is meaningful to me for this vision. Saturn alerts me to quests of my Authentic Soul in this Incarnation at this time. It keeps me on target, ruthlessly, but in love. Exploring the Life and times of Richard the Lionhearted gives me clues to a Past Life incarnation connected to this Lifetime and the journey of my Incarnate Self.

Take the symbols you saw as your Treasure and interpret their meanings according to what they connect with for you.

The Grand Staircase of Infinite Atzilut

 What did you experience as the stairs dissipated?

 What did you experience with your first breath coming back?

Your Incarnate Self in Harmony With Your Authentic Soul

SA – Your Intellect and Emotions

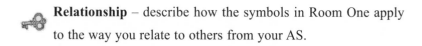 **Relationship** – describe how the symbols in Room One apply to the way you relate to others from your AS.

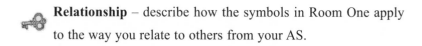 **Pathway** – describe how the symbols in Room Two apply to the way your Authentic Soul guides your Pathway in this incarnation (Lifetime), at this time.

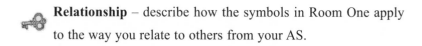 **Essence** – describe how the symbols and the word you received in Room Three apply to your deepest sense of your Incarnate Self in harmony with your Authentic Soul.

Treasure – describe how the Treasure in Room Four applies to you in this Lifetime – what is the gift it gives to you to help you stay in harmony with your Authentic Soul?

PA – Physical Assiyah

Your physical Elemental Body is a body of action.

1. How do these keys of your Authentic Soul, the symbols in each room, **guide your actions** in this incarnation?

Relationships

In what ways do you express your deepest Soul to others in this Lifetime?

Pathway

How has your pathway been guided in this Lifetime by your Authentic Soul in the light of the symbols you were shown?

What were you shown about your Pathway at this time or of the future?

 Essence

How do you put the word you received into action in your Life?

Treasure

What actions do you take to manifest the Treasure of your Authentic Soul through your Incarnate Self?

2. How do the symbols of each room relate to your physical body?

 **Relationships**

 Pathway

 Essence

Treasure

3. Where in your body (PA) do you experience the most illnesses or injuries?

Note: if you have a chronic illness or major injury, focus upon these messages. If you are illness and injury free, celebrate your harmony of AS and IS... Also look a little deeper, this may indicate that your memory may have some messages for you.

4. What is the message your Authentic Soul is sending to you through these illness and injuries to help you bring harmony to your Life?

5. As you open your consciousness to your Authentic Soul here are some keys to help you apply what you have learned:

All of the Relationships in Room One are you. Among the infinite possibilities of Being there is one dominant Key for you in this Incarnation.

All of the Pathways are you in Room Two. Among the Pathways possible, you have chosen this one Pathway Key for the purposes of this Incarnation.

All the images dancing in the mirrors in Room Three are you! However, for this Incarnation, you are in harmony best with the vibrations and rhythms of the one Essence Key with which you entered.

All of the Treasures in Room Four are symbols of your differentiation – your Authentic Soul. But one Treasure Key is the Divine Mystery unfolding through you in this Incarnation.

The Grand Staircase is Universal. It is for each of us.

As you ascend the Grand Staircase you are led to The Source, Undifferentiated Being.

As you descend the Grand Staircase you experience your individuality, the multiplicity of Creation, your own Authentic Soul.

This is your Joy of Being!

Awaken each day and say, "I love being me! It is so much fun!

I AM !

Notes

Angel Wisdoms

Each day for the next thirty days use these wisdom sayings to help you remember to center your consciousness in your Authentic Soul, uplift you and encourage you. Archangel MichaEL invites you to use the following "doorways" for daily meditation:

The Angels and I bless you as you grow and glow.

1. If you can ponder the possibility of an idea, the manifestation of it is within you and between you and others.

2. Take time each day to acknowledge who you are, where you are going, and how you desire to live your Life to your highest intentions.

3. We would have you find the **ease** of your Life.

4. Ask, and it comes to you.

5. Be. Then Do from your Being.

6. Let the Power of The Universe move in your Life.

7. Know Grace. Let go and let it come. Say Thank you!

8. Trust Divine Order.

9. Begin to hear within and TRUST.

10. See God's timing – it is everything.

11. Do not hide who you truly are. Admit it freely – to yourself and to others.

12. Begin living what you believe.

13. Be true to you, and then you will be true to others.

14. Remember who you are: an emanation of God, Love made manifest.

15. Without guilt, let go of anything inauthentic in your Life.

16. Let the Angels help you heal any situation in your Life that needs healing.

17. The Angels love to intervene for the Light in this Dimension, give them your permission by asking them to help you often!

18. Everyone has energy boundaries. To honor your energy boundaries by staying within them and not extending yourself beyond them in your choices is to honor your Authentic Soul, the Glory of The Shining Light of God.

19. Living 'well' means living in harmony with your Authentic Soul. Living from your Authentic Soul does not negate your Incarnate Self, but enhances the human experience, celebrating your Incarnate Self as a Mortal Portal.

20. The Mortal Portal gives thanks for Life, by taking advantage of the opportunities to bring Light to this planet through that Life.

21. Balance in your Life does not mean the equal distribution of work, play, meditation and exercise, but employing the needed amount of each to create harmony in your Life.

22. Whatsoever you do, do in joy with playfulness.

23. Astrological signs are for times and seasons. Your Authentic Soul moved or transported the layer of your Soul needed into your Incarnate Self at the time when the configuration of energy in the stars and planets of this Universe were in harmony with your energy vibration for the "planting" of the seed of your Soul into your body. The configuration of the stars and planets in their energy cycle is the astrological sign under which you were born. The heavens were in the necessary configuration for your Soul to move through the Dimensions into this Dimension at the time of your birth. The planets and stars witnessed your birth into this incarnation!

24. Live through your Authentic Soul and your Authentic Soul will live through you.

25. Your Angels await your call. Speak to them today!
26. Shine! Shine! Shine! Let your Light so shine, by just being you!

27. Take every opportunity to say "I love you" today and tomorrow you will gain the opportunity to love again.

28. Be Present every moment for in each moment you receive the breath of Life from God's mouth to your mouth.

29. Peace, comfort, and joy; may these be yours as you emanate your Authentic Soul throughout your Incarnate Life.

30. The message of the Seagull: It's all a playground, you know. The whole Earth Dimension is a playground.

31. It is all in Divine Order.

Epilogue

If you find subjects within this book which you would like to dialogue with me about, or to learn more I invite you to contact me at email: REBJerusalem@yahoo.com. I am here to spiritually support you.

If you would like to order CD's of the meditations in the last chapter you can do so by contacting me at REBJerusalem@yahoo.com

You Are

I Am

God Is!

BOOKS

O books
O is a symbol of the world, of oneness and unity. In different cultures it also means the "eye", symbolizing knowledge and insight, and in Old English it means "place of love or home". O books explores the many paths of understanding which different traditions have developed down the ages, particularly those today that express respect for the planet and all of life.

For more information on the full list of over 300 titles please visit our website **www.O-books.net**

myspiritradio is an exciting web, internet, podcast and mobile phone global broadcast network for all those interested in teaching and learning in the fields of body, mind, spirit and self development. Listeners can hear the show online via computer or mobile phone, and even download their favourite shows to listen to on MP3 players whilst driving, working, or relaxing.

mySpiritRadio

Feed your mind, change your life with O Books, The O Books radio programme carries interviews with most authors, sharing their wisdom on life, the universe and everything...e mail questions and co-create the show with O Books and myspiritradio.

Just visit **www.myspiritradio.com** for more information.